WEYMOUTH & PORTLAND

THEN MEETS NOW

MAUREEN ATTWOOLL

DORSET BOOKS

First published in Great Britain in 2011

British Library Cataloguing-in-Publication Data
A CIP record for this title is available from the British Library

ISBN 978 1 871164 86 2

DORSET BOOKS
Dorset Books is a partnership between
Dorset County Council and Halsgrove
Halsgrove House,
Ryelands Business Park,
Bagley Road, Wellington, Somerset TA21 9PZ
Tel: 01823 653777   Fax: 01823 216796
email: sales@halsgrove.com

Part of the Halsgrove group of companies.
Information on all Halsgrove titles is available at: www.halsgrove.com

Printed and bound in China by Everbest Printing Co Ltd

CONTENTS

INTRODUCTION

The earliest maps of Dorset date back to Tudor times, and although cartography, the science and practice of map-making, had long been in existence, inaccuracies were inevitable in an age when surveying methods were primitive and could only carried out at ground level. Maps and charts improved over the years as commerce expanded at home and seafarers brought back knowledge from foreign voyages. By the seventeenth and eighteenth centuries numerous maps and charts were being published, these often highly decorative and costly. English county maps of the period showed the locations of towns and villages and indicated features such as hills, woods and rivers, but they rarely provided the traveller with any information about routes which would enable him to travel from place to place. It was the Ordnance Survey, set up late in the eighteenth century as the Board of Ordnance to survey and map Great Britain for military purposes, which provided the first of the detailed and accurate standardised maps that we rely on today. It is fitting that this book about Weymouth, which contains extracts of many O/S maps from the nineteenth and twentieth centuries, is published in 2011, exactly 200 years since the first Ordnance Survey map of Dorset was produced in 1811.

The majority of the maps included are of Weymouth, Portland and the surrounding villages, most of which now lie within the borough boundary. Also featured are local sections of several of the early county maps which provide interesting and perhaps lesser-known aspects of the area, such as lost place-names and shipwreck sites. A selection of sea charts of the local coastal waters is also included – the oldest of these dating back to 1693.

The earliest real town plan of Weymouth, showing streets and naming the buildings within them, appeared in the first edition of John Hutchins' *History and Antiquities of the County of Dorset* published in 1774. By the end of the eighteenth century Weymouth had found fame as King George III's favourite health and pleasure resort and street maps became a feature of the guidebooks which extolled the benefits of a stay at the seaside. Some of these guidebook maps are reproduced along with other locally published maps of the eighteenth and nineteenth centuries.

The 1811 Ordnance Survey map of Dorset was followed by a series of O/S publications which continues today. The book features a selection of these dating from mid-Victorian times through to the 1950s. Weymouth was one of the places fortunate enough to be mapped at the very large scale of 10.56 feet = 1 mile (1:500) in 1863-4 and these wonderful plans provide a wealth of detail about the town and its buildings at that time. A glance at the 1950s' 50″ = 1 mile (1:1250) maps will be a reminder of the changes which have taken place over the last half century.

The boundaries of Weymouth and Melcombe Regis (originally separate towns until they were united in 1571 to form one borough) have been extended over the centuries and since 1933 have included the villages of Wyke Regis, Preston and Sutton Poyntz, Radipole, Broadwey and Upwey. Portland became part of the renamed 'Borough of Weymouth and Portland' in 1974. They, too, are represented.

It is sometimes difficult to do justice to these splendid maps as many have had to be drastically reduced in size and scale – the originals often being up to four feet wide. As with all good maps in the days before sat-nav technology, some have been deeply creased by the many hands which have unfolded and folded them over the centuries. I hope where extracts have been used they provide a sample of the information which can be gleaned from these fascinating documents. Accompanying the maps are pictures old and new to illustrate some of the changes the area has undergone since their publication.

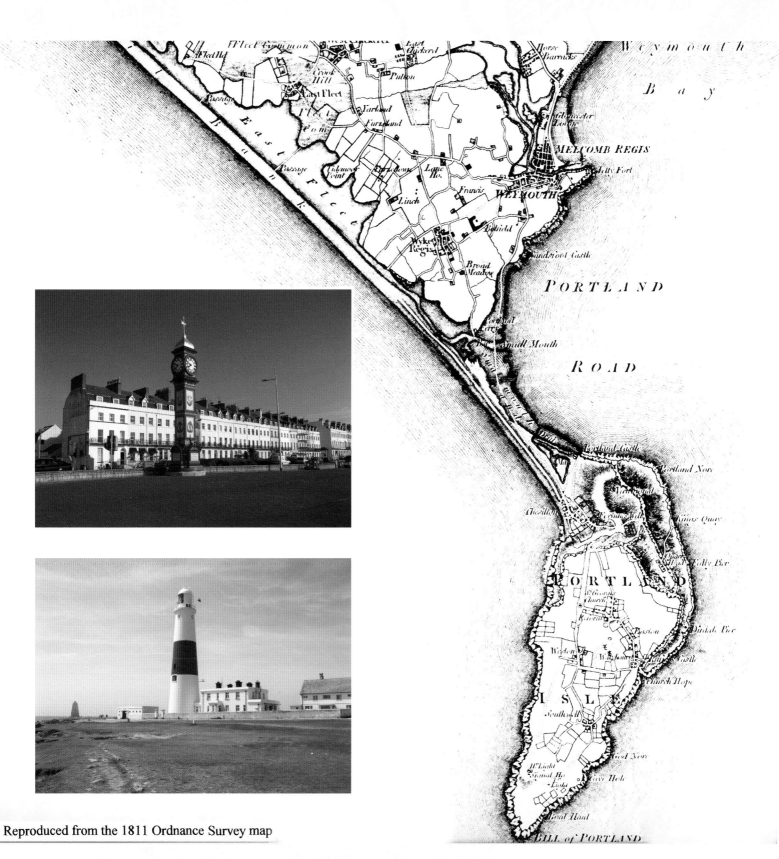

Reproduced from the 1811 Ordnance Survey map

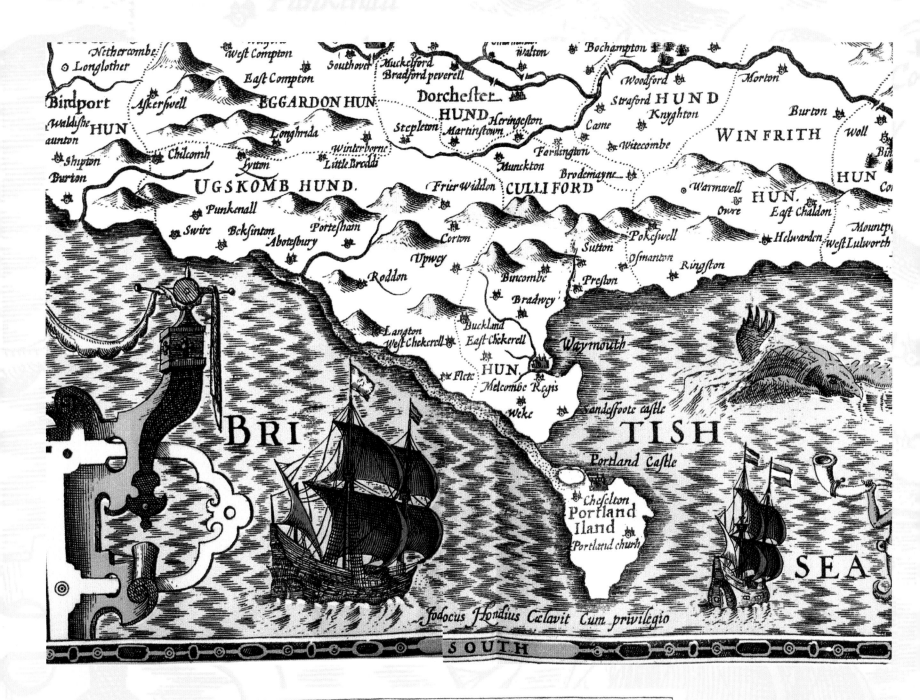

DORSETSHYRE

With the Shyre-towne Dorchester described, as also the Armes of such noble families as have bene honored with the Titles there of since the Normans Conquest to this present Anno 1610

MAP 1

JOHN SPEED'S MAP OF DORSETSHYRE, 1610

This extract showing the Weymouth and Portland area is from one of the best-known early county maps. John Speed's series of English maps of the late sixteenth and early seventeenth centuries were engraved by the famous Flemish engraver Jodocus Hondius, himself a mapmaker of note, and 'Dorsetshyre' is a fine and magnificently decorated example of his work. The dotted lines indicated the boundaries of the 'Hundreds' of the old counties. Rivers are shown and 'molehills' represent high ground. Roads did not generally appear on maps until 1675 when John Ogilby published his series of route maps.

The place names of today's towns and villages are easily recognisable, although Speed (or his engraver) has confused the locations of Weymouth and Melcombe Regis, placing them on the wrong sides of the harbour.

(Above) Speed's map shows Portland church, St Andrew's, above Church Ope Cove. The replacement of an earlier church here, it was in ruins by the time John Upham painted his views in the early nineteenth century, having been replaced by a new church, St George's, Reforne, consecrated in 1766. Pennsylvania Castle is in the background (left), the ruins of Rufus Castle on the right.

(Left) Tudor antiquarian John Leland described the church in his Itinerary – '*The Parish Church, there is but one at this time in the Isle, is long and somewhat low built in the hanging roots of a hill by the shore*'. About 100 years later Thomas Gerard of Trent wrote '*On the south point stands the only church, so near the sea that for safety of it they have been forced to wall the Churchyard Banks almost of an incredible height, so that it even afright one to look down*'.

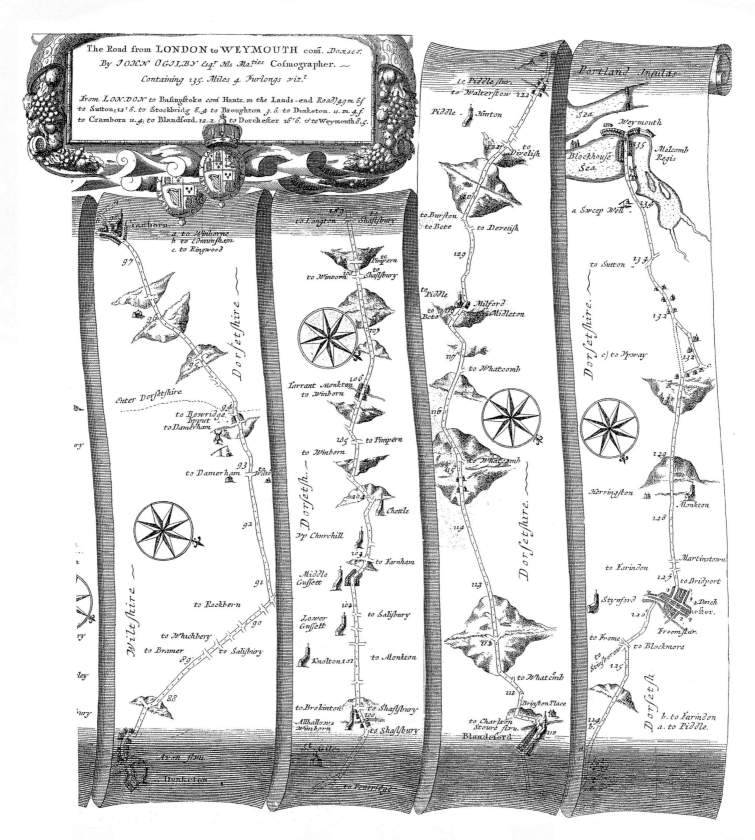

The Road from LONDON to WEYMOUTH com. Dorset.
By JOHN OGILBY Esqr His Maties Cosmographer.
Containing 135. Miles 4. Furlongs viz.t
From LONDON to Basingstoke com Hants, in the Lands-end Road) 4.9 m. 6 f.
to Sutton, 12.6. to Stockbridg 8.4 to Broughton 3.6. to Dunketon. 4. m. 4.f.
to Cramborn 11.4. to Blandford, 12.1. to Dorchester 16.6. & to Weymouth 8.5.

MAP 2

JOHN OGILBY'S LONDON TO WEYMOUTH MAP, 1675

John Ogilby was a colourful seventeenth century character who, despite several business setbacks in his earlier years, was eventually appointed 'King's Cosmographer and Geographic Printer' by King Charles II who instructed him to survey the roads of England. It was Ogilby's idea, quite revolutionary at the time, to produce a new sort of map, less ornate but far more useful than earlier costly and decorative maps which located and named settlements but provided the traveller with scant information about the roads and tracks which linked them. Ogilby designed scrolling ribbon maps which could easily be followed left-to-right, bottom-to-top on each scroll, with main roads, cross roads, place names and distances from the starting point clearly indicated along the route. He published the series of 100 maps in his *Britannia* atlas of 1675 and they are not unlike the maps motoring organisations supplied to help drivers plan their journeys in the days before sat-nav technology.

The illustration shows the second half of Ogilby's London to Weymouth map, joining the traveller as he leaves Wiltshire and enters Dorset (the numbers, which start at the bottom and end at the top of each strip, indicate the miles travelled from London ; Ogilby used the standard mile of 1760 yards at a time when local variations on the length of a mile were not uncommon). Each of his maps is accompanied by an informative description of the route and a useful guide to turnings which should be avoided along the way. Weymouth is described in some detail in the accompanying text, reproduced here as the road leaves Dorchester (shown near the base of the last 'ribbon' on the page) :-

'Leaving *Dorchester* you pass between *Monketon* Church on the Right and *Herringston* House on the Left each distant 2 Furlongs, then at 125' 6. ascending 3 Furlongs, and at 126' 7. descending 4 Furlongs; omitting the forward way on the Left which unites again at 129 miles, you pass by several scattering Houses, and after by a *Sweep*-Well on the Left, and a Wind-Mill on the Right, entring *Melcombe Regis* at 131' 7. joyn'd to *Weymouth* by a Bridg of Wood, they are seated on an arm of the Sea, formerly 2 Corporations, but by their unwearied Suits were by Act of Parliament *Tempore Eliz*. Incorporated in one by the Name of a Mayor, Aldermen *etc*. both Towns had very small beginning till of late by the convenience of their Harbor they are arrived to a greater Splendor, each Place sending 2 Burgesses to Parliament; in *Weymouth* the Chapel standeth on a Rock that is so steep that they ascend to it by 60 steps; they have 2 Markets Weekly, *viz. Tuesdays* and *Fridays*, and Enjoy an indifferent good Trade to *France, New-found Land,* &c'

In all, five routes into Dorset were described in the *Britannia* atlas of 1675. Following Ogilby's exact directions now would be almost impossible as many of what were classed as 'roads' in the late seventeenth century have disappeared under later developments or have become mere tracks today. Some place names are unrecognisable – his 'Churchill' is Crichel and 'Milford' is Milborne. One drawback for the traveller in Ogilby's day was the size and weight of the atlas, but some fifty years later another cartographer, Emanuel Bowen, produced a revised and corrected 'pocket edition' based on Ogilby's work.

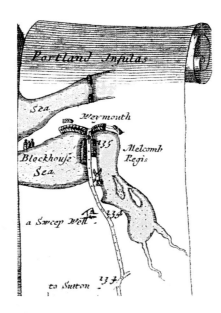 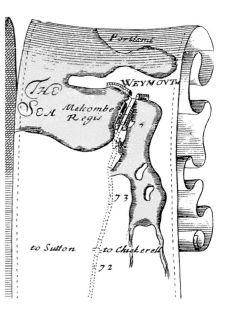

Weymouth, as shown on Ogilby's London to Weymouth map (left) and Bristol to Weymouth map (right). The sketches differ slightly and although rather quaint are interesting in that both show a windmill on what is today the Esplanade and old town records describe a windmill in this location (in the vicinity of Gloucester Lodge). The London to Weymouth map also includes a well, described as a Sweep Well, on the approach to the town.

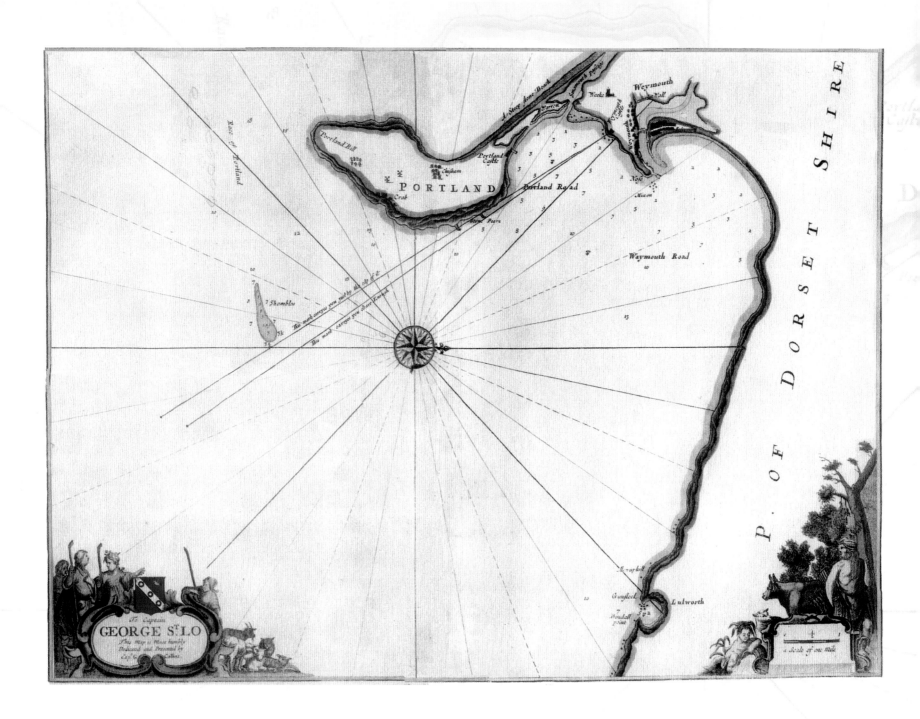

SHIRE

P. OF DORSET SHIRE

P. OF DORSET

PORTLAND

Portland Road

Weymouth Road

Race of Portland

Portland Bill

Portland Castle

Shambles

Weymouth

To Captain
GEORGE St LO

Lulworth

a Scale of one mile

MAP 3

GREENVILE COLLINS' SEA CHART, 1693

In 1681 English naval officer Captain Greenvile Collins was appointed by Samuel Pepys, Secretary to the Admiralty, to survey Britain's coasts and harbours. Collins' collection of charts was published in 1693 as *Great Britain's Coasting Pilot*, the forerunner of today's superbly detailed Admiralty Charts produced by the United Kingdom Hydrographic Office at Taunton.

Collins' chart pre-dates the first Portland lighthouses, which were not built until 1715.

Using Weymouth [Sandsfoot] Castle as his fixed point on the coast he suggests two passages by which vessels might avoid the dangerous Shambles bank – his first mark *'carryes you just by the edg of it'*, the second *'carryes you cleare Enough'*.

Portland's two ancient windmills are depicted; the village of Chiswell or Chesil is named as *'Chisham'* and *'A Steep Stone Bank'* describes Chesil Beach. Interestingly, *'a Wall'* is shown at Weymouth which must have been an early attempt to prevent the sea flooding today's Marsh area.

The map is dedicated to Captain George St Lo, a commissioner of the navy, whose service record was somewhat tarnished in 1697 when he was ordered to guard and assist the men constructing the first Eddystone lighthouse. He sailed out of Plymouth in HMS *Terrible* to join the fleet, leaving the workforce and the lighthouse's architect unprotected on the rock and at the mercy of a French privateer which carried them all off. They were released soon afterwards but St Lo received a sharp reprimand for neglecting orders.

Weymouth, enlarged from Collins' 1693 chart.

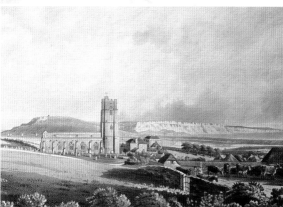

Wyke, or 'Weeke' church, another well-known sea mark, is shown on the chart .

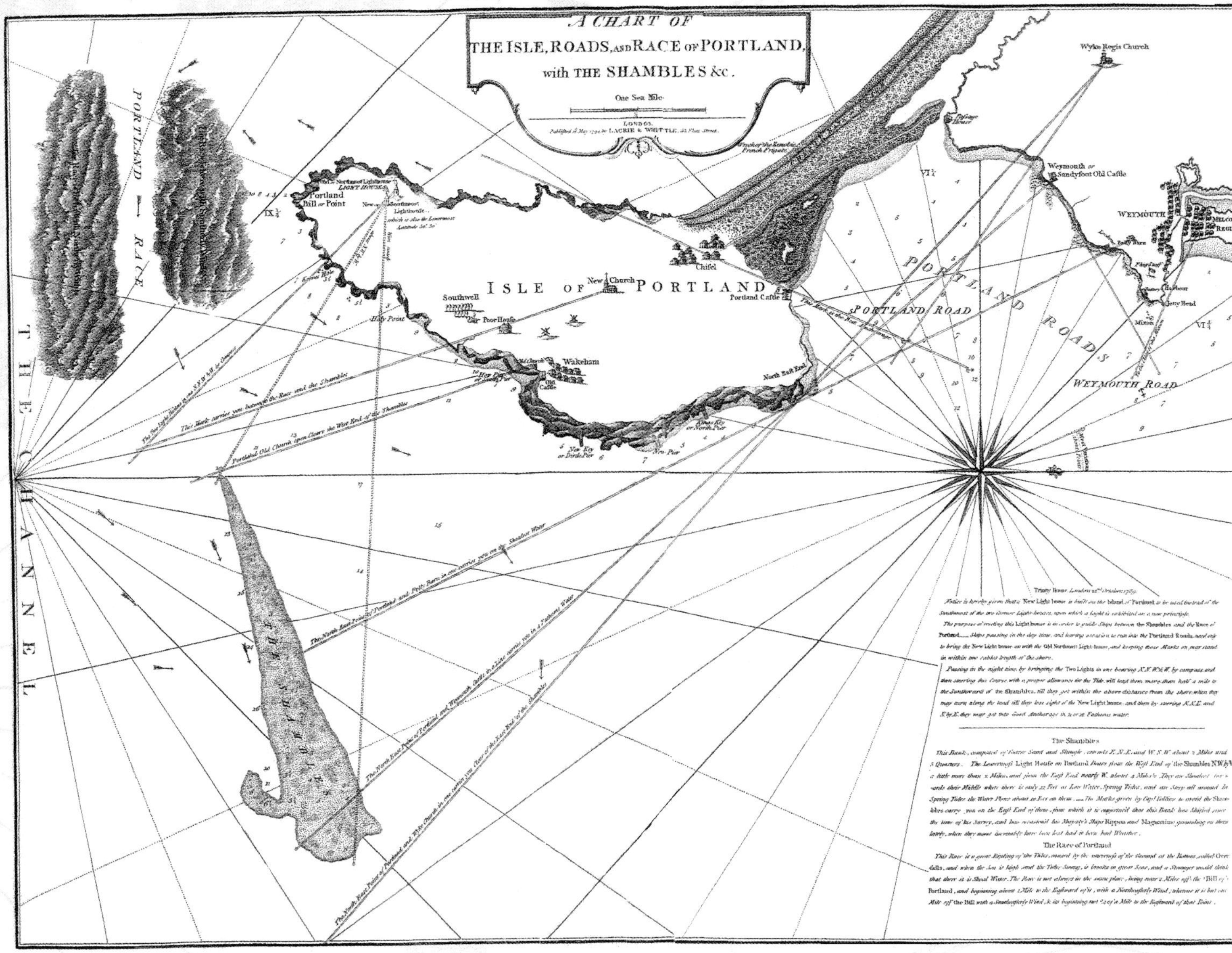

MAP 4

LAURIE AND WHITTLE'S SEA CHART, 1794

Navigating the waters around Portland is no easy task today and this complex chart of 1794, another forerunner of the detailed Admiralty charts which would follow, was published by Laurie and Whittle. Laurie later joined the well known sea chart publishing firm of Imrie, Laurie, Norie and Wilson.

The accompanying text is reproduced here – the 'new lighthouse' of 1789 had replaced the original Lower Light of 1715 and both the Upper and Lower Lights shown on the chart were replaced in the 1860s. The two

Victorian structures still stand, although the present lighthouse at the Bill rendered them both redundant in 1906. The Shambles bank and Portland Race are shown on the chart, the notes clearly emphasising the dangers here.

'Folly Barn' is a landmark on the Weymouth side of Portland Roads and it appears to have stood somewhere in the Rodwell/Chapelhay district. Sandsfoot Castle (rather engagingly referred to on some of these early maps as 'Sandyfoot Castle') and the tower of Wyke church have long been points of reference for those at sea.

The Shambles

This Bank, composed of Coarse Sand and Shingle, extends E.N.E. and W.S.W. about 2 Miles and 3 Quarters. The Lowermost Light House on Portland Bears from the West End of the Shambles NWbyW a little more than 2 Miles, and from the East End nearly W. about 4 Miles½. They are Shoalest towards their Middle where there is only 12 Feet at Low Water, Spring Tides, and are Steep all around. In Spring Tides the Water Flows about 10 Feet on them. — The Marks given by Capt. Collins to avoid the Shambles carry you on the East End of them, from which it is conjectured that this Bank has Shifted since the time of his Survey, and has occasiond his Majesty's Ships Rippon and Magnanime grounding on them lately, when they must inevitably have been lost had it been bad Weather.

The Race of Portland

This Race is a great Ripling of the Tides, caused by the uneveness of the Ground at the Bottom, called Overfalls, and when the Sea is high, and the Tides Strong, it breaks in great Seas, and a Stranger would think that there it is Shoal Water. The Race is not always in the same place, being near 2 Miles off the Bill of Portland, and beginning about 1 Mile to the Eastward of it, with a Northeasterly Wind; whereas it is but one Mile off the Bill with a Southeasterly Wind, & its beginning not ¾ of a Mile to the Eastward of that Point.

Trinity House, London 22nd October 1789.

Notice is hereby given that a New Light house is built on the Island of Portland, to be used instead of the Southmost of the two former Light-houses, upon which a Light is exhibited on a new principle.

The purpose of erecting this Light-house is in order to guide Ships between the Shambles and the Race of Portland — Ships passing in the day time, and having occasion to run into the Portland Roads, need only to bring the New Light house on with the Old Northmost Light-house, and keeping those Marks on, may stand in within two cables length of the shore.

Passing in the night time, by bringing the Two Lights in one bearing N.N.W.½W. by compass, and then steering this Course, with a proper allowance for the Tide, will lead them more than half a mile to the Southward of the Shambles, till they get within the above distance from the shore; when they may turn along the land till they lose sight of the New Light house; and then by steering N.N.E. and N.by E. they may get into Good Anchorage in 11 or 12 Fathoms water.

The two lighthouses shown above are those of 1715 - the original Lower Light (left) and the Higher Light (right).

(Above, left) The Lower Light was replaced in 1789 by the structure above (the new one referred to on the chart). (Above, right) William Daniell's watercolour is of the old Higher Light in the days when Portland was famous for its mutton and sheep grazed on the cliffs at the Bill.

(Middle) Both lighthouses were rebuilt in the 1860s.

(Bottom) Shown under construction, the present red-banded lighthouse replaced the Victorian buildings in 1906, although they still stand – the Lower Light is now a bird observatory and the Upper has been converted to residential use.

them lies
Horsepool
Gate Linton Hill
Farm
The
Swan
Guns Gate
Wall
Down
Roddon
Skelvington
Dairy
House
J. Floyer Esq.
Upway
W. Little Esq.
Buncom
Wyke Wood
SUTTON
Broadway
Roddon Hill
Buckland
Holwell
Wood
POINTZ
Nottington
Thornhill
Langston
Tatton Farm
West
Boat House
Herring
Buckland Ripers
CULLIFORD TREE
Gate
Chickerell
Mill
Knacker's
Hole
Parsonage
Fleet Down
Down
Lodmoor
East
Broadstone
West.
Chickerell
Radipole
Fleet
House
East
Chickerell
Fleet
The Hop a Spanish Ship
from the Spanish Main
Stranded here 30000. was
Saved out of her.
Patton
SUTTON
Turnpike
W
POINTZ
Chesil
East Fleet
LIBERTY
Barn
MELCOMB
REGIS
Yearty Lane
Harbour
Jetty
Mixon
Furse down
Lane
Francis
of
House
WEYMOUTH
Flagstone
Battery
Fleet
Lynch
Wyke
Regis
Lousy bush
Lookout
Chesil
Sandsfoot
Old Castle
Broad
mead
Bank
Passage
House
Port land
Road
Portland
Castle
The
Mare
New
Quarry
Chesil
Wreck of the
Zenobie F. Frigate
Motains
Fancones
Well

REMARK

The Stones on the Chisle Bank lessen in Size gradually
to the Westward from Portland; At Chisle & the Passage, they
are about the size of an Egg. opposite Fleet & Langston,
they are much smaller, at Becksington they are scarcely
bigger than Pease, & between Swyre & Burton-cliffe where
the Bank ends it is entirely a fine clear Sand. Underneath
the Pebbles is a firm Black Clay, which appears when a
Strong S.E: Wind blows. the Bank is then swept (from one
End to the other) of the Stones, and remains only of Clay
till Such time a S.W. Wind blows, when the Sea throws
them up & covers the Bank again. This Bank is 16¾ Miles
in length.

MAP 5

ISAAC TAYLOR'S DORSETSHIRE MAP, 1765

Isaac Taylor's 1765 map is important in the history of the mapping of Dorset as it is the first large-scale map of the county (1″ = 1 mile). Although he has been criticised for some of its inaccuracies the map shows roads in some detail and includes the then newly established Turnpike Trusts. Taylor knew the county well, having already mapped the estates of several Dorset landowners. His map is extremely large – 5 feet x almost 4 feet (152 x 112 cm) and highly decorative. Unusually, it indicates the sites of three contemporary shipwrecks on Chesil Beach. The loss of the *Hope* near Fleet in 1749 led to one of Dorset's most notorious cases of wholesale plundering of cargo from a wrecked vessel. Again, in 1762 when the French vessel *Zenobie* went ashore close to Portland with some 200 men aboard, many were drowned and those who survived were 'robbed and stripped by the natives' to such an extent that they were clothed and sent back to France on the orders of the King instead of being treated as prisoners of war. A little further west and not shown on the extract, the *Squirrel* was wrecked in 1750, although dated as 1748 on the map. Taylor's description of the grading of the Chesil Beach pebbles is included.

Along with the today's town and village names, many familiar place-names in the Weymouth area appear on the map such as Lynch, Lane House, Francis and Broadmead. Less familiar and not at all picturesque are others such as 'Lousy Bush' in the Wyke/Rodwell area and 'Knackers Hole' at Redlands. At Upwey Taylor adds the names of the important occupiers of a couple of the larger houses there – J. Floyer Esq. at Westbrook House and W. Lisle Esq. at Upwey Manor (this was Warren Lisle of HM Customs service). Note that in 1765 Taylor used the ending 'way' for Upway and Broadway although choosing the more modern version of Weymouth. Dorset's Turnpike Trusts date from about the middle of the 18th century and Taylor depicts the Turnpike Gate which then stood at the north end of Melcombe (in the vicinity of the present St John's church).

'Sandyfoot [Sandsfoot] Old Castle', the disused fortification dating from King Henry VIII's time and built on crumbling cliffs was in a semi-ruinous state by 1765, the locals having been given permission to remove its stones for their own building work once its days as a defence work were over. The Passage House at Wyke was where folk wanting to cross to Portland waited for the tethered ferry which took them across Smallmouth, the opening at the eastern end of the Fleet water. The whole of this coast would suffer extensive damage in the 'Great Gale' of 22nd/23rd November 1824 and in that terrible storm the ferryman was drowned and the passage by water here was considerably widened by the force of the sea. A temporary ferry served the island for 15 years before it was linked to the mainland by the first Ferrybridge in 1839. This first wooden bridge was replaced in the 1890s by a steel structure, but it too has now vanished, as has the original Smallmouth passage, for the present road bridge of 1984 was built nearer to Portland and the Fleet water was diverted to flow under it, the original passage then being filled in.

Looking from Portland to the Passage House at Wyke, with Wyke church in the background. The print on the left is from John Love's collection of local views, published in 1790. The similar view on the right is by an unnamed artist.

This painting probably dates to around 1865 and shows the original wooden viaduct which carried the trains of the Weymouth and Portland Railway across Smallmouth. On the right is the first bridge which took road traffic to Portland, opened in 1839 and also a timber structure. Both these bridges would later be replaced by steel bridges which have also gone – the steel rail bridge of the early 1900s being demolished in the 1971, some ten years after the railway finally closed and the road bridge of the 1890s being replaced by the present Ferrybridge which opened in 1984. (*See* MAPS 41 and 42 *for illustrations of the more recent history of the Ferrybridges*)

An AUTHENTICK

ACCOUNT

OF THE

HOPE,

A VERY RICH

Dutch Merchant-Ship

Laden with Money and Goods,

THAT WAS

Caft-away on PORTLAND-BEACH

IN THE

County of DORSET,

The 16th of *January*, 1748.

WITH THE

Manner of her being plunder'd by a vaft Con-
courfe of PEOPLE.

AND THE

Trial at large of *A. Elliott*, who was tried at the Af-
fizes held at *Dorchefter* the 15th of *July*, 1749,
for felonioufly carrying away Part of her Cargoe.

By a GENTLEMAN in the Neighbourhood.

LONDON:

Printed for A. WEBB, near St. *Paul's*, and Sold by the
Bookfellers. M.DCC.XLIX
[Price Four-Pence.]

Publications about local shipwrecks were best sellers – this was the account of the *Hope*, lost in 1749. Augustin Elliott of Portland was found not guilty of stealing part of the cargo, which was perhaps not surprising since most of the local population descended on the beach to search for and make off with the large amount of gold the vessel was said to be carrying. Some of the looters may even have served on the jury! The publication dates the wreck to 1748, which is 1749 in modern dating. It was 1752 before the start of the year was standardised as 1st January and when this publication appeared both old and new calendars were in use. The author has used the old calendar, when the new year did not begin until 25th March.

SERIOUS ADVICE

AND

FAIR WARNING

To all that live upon the Sea-Coaft
of *England* and *Wales*,

PARTICULARLY

To thofe in the Neighbourhood of *Weymouth* and *Portland*;

Addreffed to them in

SERMON

Preached the 22d of *December*, 1754,
in the Churches of *Fleet* and *Chickerill*,
on Occafion of feveral Shipwrecks at that
Time upon the Coaft of *England*.

To which are added,

Some Extracts from the feveral Acts of
Parliament relating to Ships that are ftranded
on the Coaft, and the Penalties to be inflicted
on all thofe that plunder the Merchants Goods.

By THOMAS FRANCKLYN,

Rector of *Langton-Herring*, and Vicar of *Fleet*
in the County of *Dorfet*.

LONDON

Printed for A. LINDE, in *Catherine-Street* in the
Strand. M.DCC.LVI.

Priests in coastal parishes were required to preach a sermon four times a year warning their congregations of the penalties which could be incurred for looting wrecked vessels. Judging from some of the incidents which occurred locally later in the eighteenth century, Thomas Francklyn's advice went largely unheeded.

Sandsfoot Castle in 1756. Built in 1539, it had not been used as a defence work since the mid-seventeenth century and had already lost some of its stonework to local building projects.

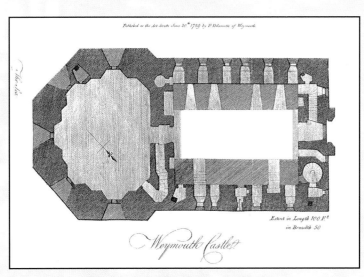

A plan of Sandsfoot Castle as first completed, taken from a local guidebook of 1780.

In the days of the Turnpike Trusts the local road to Smallmouth ran down what is today Old Castle Road and along the foreshore below Sandsfoot Castle.

A picnic spot and popular picture postcard view in the early 1900s.

A 1960s' view – there had been a substantial fall of masonry onto the beach below in the mid-1950s.

Sandsfoot Castle, undergoing extensive conservation work in 2011.

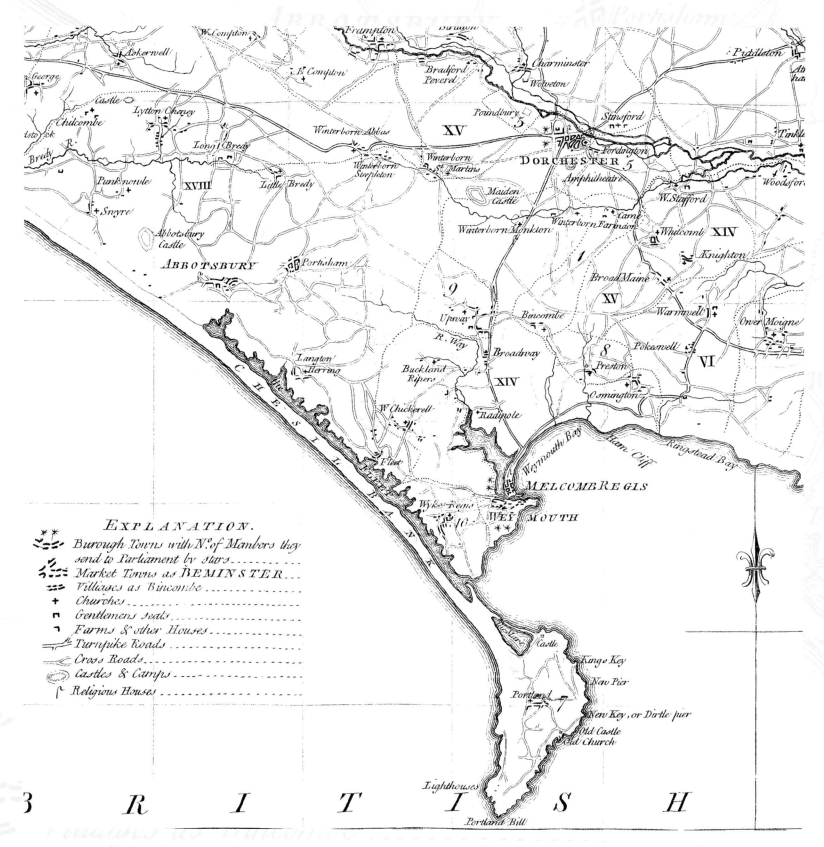

EXPLANATION.

⁂ Burough Towns with N.º of Members they
send to Parliament by stars ....
Market Towns as BEMINSTER ...
Villages as Bincombe ....
✝ Churches ....
Gentlemens seats ....
Farms & other Houses ....
Turnpike Roads ....
Cross Roads ....
Castles & Camps ....
Religious Houses ....

MAP 6

JOHN BAYLY'S MAP OF DORSETSHIRE, 1773

This extract is taken from '*A Map of Dorsetshire from Actual Surveys and Records of the County*, by J. Bayly, 1773', the whole county map being the frontispiece of the first edition of John Hutchins' *The History and Antiquities of the County of Dorset*, published in 1774. Since that date Hutchins' work has become the standard history of the county, but alas, the Dorset-born cleric and Rector of Wareham died in 1773 just months before its publication, so never saw his great life's work in print. Eleven years earlier his manuscript had almost been lost when fire swept through Wareham, destroying the Rectory and most of its contents. Hutchins was away at Swyre, his other parish, and it was his wife who rescued his Dorset research papers before fleeing the blaze.

A second edition of the *History* was published between 1796 and 1815 and expanded the original work from two to four volumes, and a third four-volume edition was published as a part-work from 1861 to 1874, some printings of these two editions also being available as large paper copies. The third edition was reprinted in the early 1970s. A unique 'Grangerised' version of the large-paper second edition is now in the Dorset History Centre, the text of its original four volumes having been expanded to fourteen leather-bound tomes with the addition of numerous maps, illustrations, letters and other original material collected and arranged in the early 1900s by Alexander Meyrick Broadley of Bradpole, a wealthy collector of Dorsetiana.

Bayly's map shows the steep 'Old Roman Road' which was the route from Upwey to Dorchester prior to the cutting of a new road in 1824, with gentler gradients but a sharply angled hairpin bend (*see* MAP 59) – this part of the A354 road now replaced by the 2011 Relief Road. The old road heads up from the centre of this early 1900s picture of Upwey; the gypsy caravan is starting the climb to the hairpin bend. The pub on the right is the Royal Oak, demolished in 1968.

Bayly's map only appears in the first edition of 1774 and shows the turnpike road system which by then had been in existence for some twenty years and was still expanding. 'Stars' around towns indicate the number of Members of Parliament elected in each town – two in Dorchester and a staggering total of four in Weymouth and Melcombe Regis, a throwback to the days when the Borough had been two separate towns. This anomaly, which turned the town into a political 'prize' and led to a great deal of vote rigging, did not end until the Reform Act of 1832 when the number of MPs was reduced to two. In 1885 Weymouth lost the right to elect its own MP and became part of the South Dorset constituency.
(*For the town maps of Weymouth which were published in Hutchins'* History, *see* MAPS 9 *and* 10; *Portland, see* MAP 43)

The last of the old local turnpike buildings, long since converted to residential use was demolished in 1972. It stood on Dorchester Road at Radipole.

MAP 7

THE FIRST ORDNANCE SURVEY MAP OF DORSET, 1811

In the 1760s proposals were put forward to make an official survey of Great Britain for military purposes, but 1791 is the generally accepted date for the foundation of the government department known today as the Ordnance Survey, taking its name from the original army Board of Ordnance. Early in the 1800s the first maps were published in what became known as the 'One-inch series' (1″ = 1 mile or 1: 63,360) eventually mapping the entire country. This was the beginning of standardisation in mapping, and an accurate depiction of the road systems at that time.

Dorset's first 1″ O/S map was published in 1811 and the section opposite is of the Weymouth and Portland area. This 200-year old fine copper plate engraving of the First Edition is rather heavily inked but the attention to detail is obvious even on this small extract of the county map.

Just above the word Wakeham, almost in the centre of the Portland map, can be seen the towers of the only two remaining (although long disused) windmills in Dorset. They date at least to the beginning of the seventeenth century and are listed buildings. On the right, the South Mill has some holes in the stonework at lower level, made when the tower was used by the Home Guard during The Second World War. The photographs were taken in 1973.

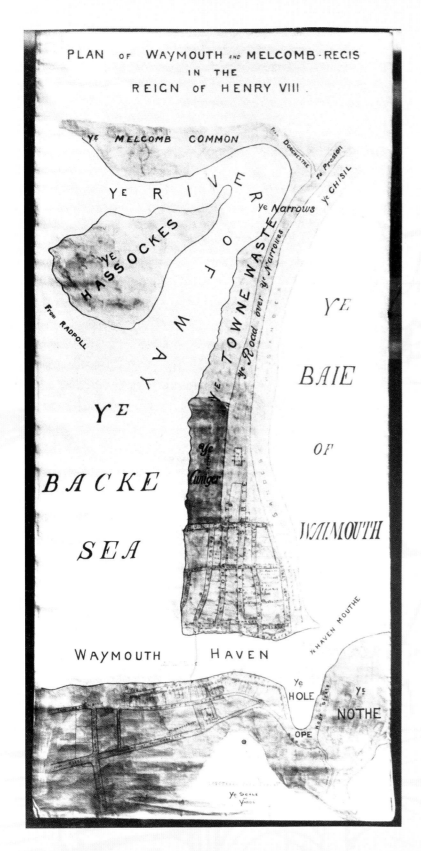

Few sixteenth and seventeenth century buildings exist in the town centre. This one stood on the corner of Church Passage (site of the current No. 45 St Mary Street), and was demolished in 1883.

Some Tudor buildings have survived ; these are the Tudor cottages in Trinity Street, which can be visited at specified times.

MAP 8

THE 'TUDOR' MAP OF WEYMOUTH (1533)

Moving now into town plans of Weymouth, the earliest such map and its origins remain something of a mystery. It first appears to have been published in Miss E. S. L. Cosens' *A short history of Weymouth for the use of schools,* an excellent little history of the town which was published locally by Sherren and Son in 1927. The map, as reproduced in the book, appears to be of some age. Miss Cosens does not acknowledge its source, so whether it is of Tudor date or was compiled later from town records is yet to be discovered. There is much use of 'Ye' rather than the modern 'The' on the map and although its title is PLAN OF WAYMOUTH AND MELCOMB REGIS IN THE REIGN OF HENRY VIII, the heading may have been added at a later date. Leaving its origins aside, the map does appear to be a fair representation of the town at that time. Miss Cosens captioned it *Weymouth in Leland's time (1533)* and it is a useful guide to the layout of the two towns in the sixteenth century in the years shortly before the separate and quarrelsome boroughs of Weymouth and Melcombe Regis were ordered to unite and become a single borough in 1571.

It shows the harbour (Waymouth Haven) in the days prior to the construction of the first Town Bridge of the 1590s, when a ferryboat was the only means of crossing the water between Melcombe Regis (the end of St Nicholas Street) and Weymouth (today's North Quay). Ancient Melcombe street names are shown – St Nicholas Strete, St Thomas Strete, St Mary Strete, Mayden Strete and so on. At the south end of the 'Ye Baie of Waimouth' is the place where 'all ye rubbish of ye town is caste'.

At the top of the map 'Ye Hassocks' was then an island in 'Ye Backe Sea', where much modern reclamation has taken place. 'Ye Melcombe Common' (sometimes referred to as Clark's Hill) is now the Westerhall district and 'Ye Chisil' represents Preston Beach, 'cesil' being an ancient word for shingle or pebble.

Across the 'haven' Weymouth streets run west to east along the harbour side, much restricted by the high ground behind. They include St Nicholas Street, which was later renamed Chapelhay Street to avoid confusion with the street of the same name in Melcombe. High Street in Tudor times ran right along the south harbourside to 'Ope'. Today this stretch of old High Street from the Town Bridge to Hope Square is known as Trinity Road, leading into Trinity Street.

By the end of the sixteenth century a timber bridge had been built across Weymouth Harbour to replace the old ferry. No contemporary illustrations exist, but Eric Ricketts' drawing has been made from written records of the period. The view looks across the water from the Melcombe side and the building shown on the high ground in Weymouth is the mediaeval chapel of St Nicholas. The chapel, which is the origin of the name 'Chapelhay', was used as a fort and damaged beyond repair in the Civil War fighting of the 1640s.

In the mid-nineteenth century the original Holy Trinity School was built on the chapel's site, at the top of the present Chapelhay Steps, but the school, too, fell victim to war – this time the air raids of World War Two, which destroyed so much of the Chapelhay area. Some years later the houses shown here, Trinity Court, were built on this historic site.

MAP 9

MAP OF WEYMOUTH AND MELCOMBE REGIS

From John Hutchins' *The History and Antiquities of the County of Dorset.* **1st Edition, published in 1774 (Volume 1, page 400)**

1774 saw the publication of the first edition of what was to become the most important work on the county's history – John Hutchins' *The History and Antiquities of the County of Dorset* (*see* MAP 6 *for the history of Hutchins' various editions*).

This map appeared in the two-volume first edition of the *History* and is the earliest known detailed 'street plan' of Weymouth, showing both streets and buildings. Horse-drawn bathing machines can be seen on the sands, a sign that the town was already established as a health and pleasure resort. One suspects that this map was commissioned some time before publication of the *History* in 1774, as the cartographer has not extended his map very much beyond the town's main streets: had it been contemporary with publication, the map would surely have featured the new Stacie's Hotel of 1773, built on what was then open ground to the north, where the later Esplanade terraces would also be built. Stacie's later became known as the first 'Royal Hotel', and provided purpose-built accommodation for wealthy visitors, who, if they were not invited to stay with the local gentry, had previously only had the choice of the town centre coaching inns or lodging houses.

Assembly Rooms were an essential feature of any resort and 'Delamotte's Publick Rooms' are featured, where society gathered to dance, play cards, gossip and be entertained. These, though, were on the south side of the harbour beside the yet to be filled-in inlet which became Hope Square. They lost popularity when Stacie's Assembly Rooms opened in the new hotel on the sea front, after which Delamotte's became known, as they are today, as the 'Old Rooms', in Trinity Street.

The expense of preparing the map was borne by William Chafin Grove and Gabriel Steward, both influential property owners in the town, who represented Weymouth and Melcombe Regis in Parliament in the late eighteenth century.

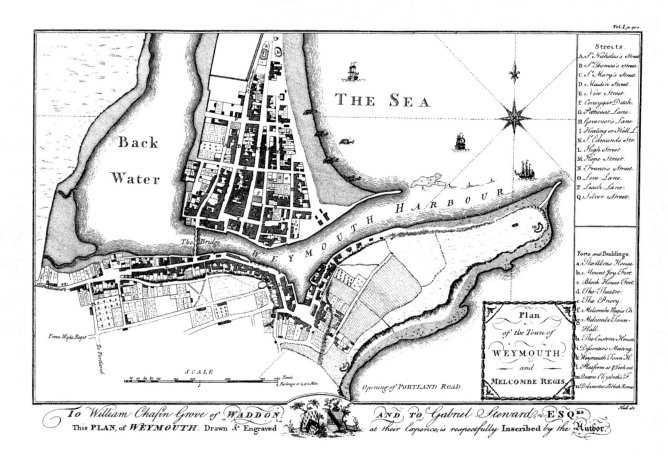

MAP 10

MAP OF WEYMOUTH AND MELCOMBE REGIS

From John Hutchins' *The History and Antiquities of the County of Dorset*. 2nd Edition, published in 1803 (Volume 2, page 62)

Between 1796 and 1815 a second edition of John Hutchins' *History* was published. Hutchins was long dead and this new edition was enlarged to 4 volumes and edited by Richard Gough, who had worked on the first edition, and John Bowyer Nichols. In some copies of Volume II, published in 1803, our Weymouth map appears once again, but in curiously amended form.

Between the two editions of 1774 and 1803 the Duke of Gloucester had built Gloucester Lodge in 1780, facing the sea but north of the area shown on the map. The gardens of his house (King George III's residence during his Weymouth holidays) reached down as far as today's School Street and the large empty space shown on the west side of Melcombe on the first edition of the map has been filled with trees and shrubs to indicate that this ground was now part of the royal gardens adjacent to the Lodge.

The second amendment on the map is a planned development which never materialised so it is difficult to understand why it has been included. The map shows a straight road along the town shore of the Backwater. It was here that local Georgian architect and builder James Hamilton put forward proposals in the 1790s to reclaim land, build a new sea wall and provide sites for houses along a planned new road skirting the back of the town. His design was never carried through. Only West Parade, the original name of a short stretch of today's Park Street behind Royal Terrace, may have been the beginnings of Hamilton's road. It was to be many years before Commercial Road, the eventual route along the back of the town, was completed and it was constructed in piecemeal fashion following later extensive Backwater reclamation. Nothing else on the original map has been altered, so the inclusion at that time of a proposed, rather than an actual road, remains something of a mystery, especially as the reclamation of the inlet on the southern side of the harbour (today's Hope Square area) is not shown although it had been infilled in 1781, more than twenty years before this volume was published.

The editors of the second edition devote several pages of text to a description of the flourishing health and pleasure resort and the frequent visits of King George III to his brother's seafront residence, yet apart from indicating the gardens of Gloucester Lodge, the map shows nothing of the developments along the Esplanade, which by 1803 was walled and very much part of the seaside scene.

This map did not appear in all versions of the second edition of 1803, and it is not always included in the various listings which have been produced of the illustrations in Hutchins' volumes. John Harvey's guidebook map of 1800, which is a more accurate representation of Weymouth at that time, was published in other versions of the 1803 Second Edition. (*See* next entry)

No map of Weymouth was included in the 4-volume third edition of Hutchins' *History*, which was published in instalments between 1861 and 1870.

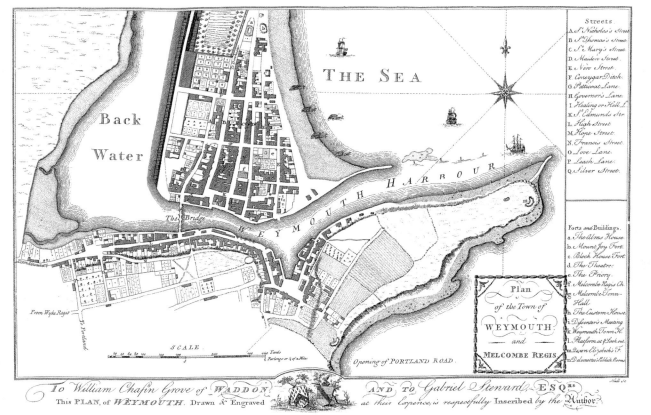

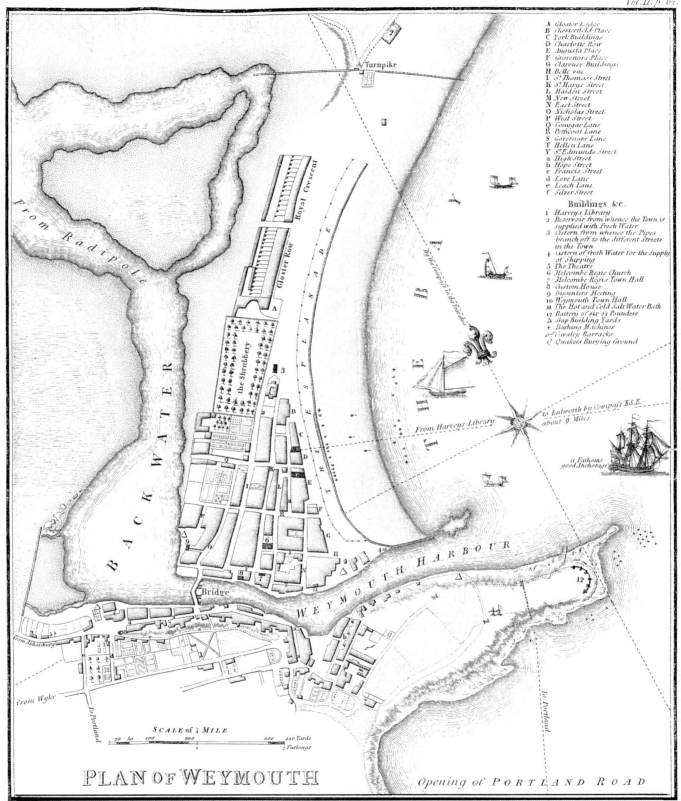

A Gloster Lodge
B Chesterfield Place
C York Buildings
D Charlotte Row
E Augusta Place
F Grovenors Place
G Clarence Buildings
H Belle vue
I St Thomas's Street
K St Marys Street
L Maiden Street
M New Street
N East Street
O Nicholas Street
P West Street
Q Conygar Lane
R Petticoat Lane
S Governors Lane
T Hellen Lane
V St Edmunds Street
a High Street
b Hope Street
c Francis Street
d Love Lane
e Leach Lane
f Silver Street

Buildings &c.

1 Harveys Library
2 Reservoir from whence the Town is
   supplied with Fresh Water
3 Cistern from whence the Pipes
   branch off to the different Streets
   in the Town
4 Cistern of Fresh Water for the Supply
   of Shipping
5 The Theatre
6 Melcombe Regis Church
7 Melcombe Regis Town Hall
8 Custom House
9 Dissenters Meeting
10 Weymouth Town Hall
11 The Hot and Cold Salt Water Bath
12 Battery of six 24 Pounders
△ Ship Building Yards
+ Bathing Machines
   Cavalry Barracks
Q Quakers Burying Ground

From Radipole

Royal Crescent

Gloster Row

the Shrubbery

ESPLANADE

THE BAY

By the Compass to the Fourth...

From Harveys Library

to Lulworth by Compass E.S.E. about 9 Miles

11 Fathoms good Anchorage

BACKWATER

Turnpike

Bridge

WEYMOUTH HARBOUR

from Abbotsbury

from Wyke

To Portland

To Portland

SCALE of ¼ MILE

20 50 100 200   400   440 Yards
                              2 Furlongs

PLAN OF WEYMOUTH

Opening of PORTLAND ROAD

MAP 11

PLAN OF WEYMOUTH

From JOHN HARVEY'S *Improved Weymouth Guide,* published in 1800

In 1800 John Harvey of Harvey's Library on Weymouth Esplanade published his *Improved Weymouth Guide* and this 'New Map of Weymouth, including the late Additions and Improvements' is its frontispiece. A very attractive and decorative map, it was drawn by J. Ham and engraved for Harvey's guidebook by B. Baker.

It is also the map that was included in some copies of the Second Edition of John Hutchins' *History* published in 1803 and it provides a far better indication of the changes brought about by sea bathing and the continuing visits of King George III than the alternative map used by the editors in some copies of the second edition (*see* previous page). The legend 'Vol. II, p.62' above the map's border refers to its placement in Hutchins.

Harvey's map shows few changes on the Weymouth side of the harbour when compared with Hutchins' map published in 1774; perhaps not surprising, as attention was now very much focused on Melcombe. It does, however, show the 1781 reclamation of the inlet which is now Hope Square.

By this date it was clear that King George III found the town very much to his liking and from 1789 he holidayed here with various members of his family almost every year. At 'A' on Harvey's map can be found the royal summer residence, Gloucester Lodge, with its gardens, known as The Shrubbery, stretching down towards the town (and later built on, providing the sites for Royal Terrace and Frederick Place in the first half of the nineteenth century). A slightly surprising omission from the 'Buildings' list is Stacie's, the leading hotel and assembly rooms in

Gloucester Row, although Harvey naturally gives prominence to his own library (and rival 'rooms') on the Esplanade.

Beyond Gloucester Row, Royal Crescent was still under construction in 1800 and it was completed as a straight terrace of 15 houses, now missing one of the original houses at its northern end where road widening took place in the early twentieth century. Local architect James Hamilton had put forward a design for Royal Crescent, but it was built on a much more modest scale than the long curved terrace of some 50 houses that he originally envisaged.

Hamilton and his associate Robert Vining were also in the process of constructing the Esplanade wall in 1800 and a line of posts and chains denotes the new pedestrian walkway along the seafront. Bathing machines – the guidebook tells us they were 'upwards of thirty in number'- are shown on the sands and in the sea.

John Harvey was one of the interesting characters of Georgian Weymouth. A prominent figure on the social scene, he was also an engineer who as early as 1794 put forward proposals for building a breakwater to enclose Portland Harbour. (*See* MAP 44 *for an illustration of his plan*) His *Improved Guide* is undated but it includes descriptions of King George III's visits to Weymouth up to 1798 and is generally assumed to have been published in 1800. If so, his map should have been available for inclusion in all copies of the 1803 second edition of Hutchins, but perhaps the editors, who had a mammoth task enlarging and updating the original work, had finished their editing of the Weymouth section long before 1800.

As can be seen on this and the two previous maps, a new Town Bridge of 1770 had changed its location and crossed the harbour at the end of St Nicholas Street instead of its traditional spot at the end of St Thomas Street. It was not a popular move, and when the first stone bridge replaced this timber structure in 1824 it reverted to the site we know today.

Seen from the present Town Bridge, old warehouses appear on both pictures. The site of the 1770 bridge was at the end of St Nicholas Street, between the pub and the last warehouse on the left. Modern apartment blocks complement the older buildings.

GLOUCESTER LODGE : HISTORY OF A ROYAL RESIDENCE

John Harvey's Map of 1800 was published during the heyday of the visits of King George III and his family and it gives due prominence to the royal residence, Gloucester Lodge, and its gardens, known as The Shrubbery. These views show some of the changes the building has undergone over more than 200 years.

The house was built in 1780 by William Henry, Duke of Gloucester, younger brother of King George III. He lent the Lodge in 1789 to King George III and Queen Charlotte, initially for the King's convalescence after his episode of so-called 'madness'. It afterwards became a regular holiday home for the King and his family (he had 13 surviving children who all visited the town at some time during the fourteen occasions the King stayed here between 1789-1805). The King bought the Lodge from his brother in 1801.

Gloucester Lodge, as first built. It was also known as Royal Lodge. The entrance was then at the side of the building, in the gardens known as 'The Shrubbery'.

THE
RESIDENCE AND FURNITURE,
CLOCKS, GLASSES, &c. &c. of
HIS LATE MAJESTY'S,
At Weymouth.
A
CATALOGUE
OF THE ENTIRE ASSEMBLAGE OF
HOUSEHOLD FURNITURE,
OF
GLOUCESTER LODGE, and Four Houses adjoining:
COMPRISING
BRILLIANT PLATE GLASSES,
Valuable and excellent Clocks, by Gulliamy, Harvey, Recordon, and Others;
PIANO-FORTES AND HARPSICHORDS, BY KIRKMAN AND OTHERS:
BAROMETERS & THERMOMETERS, BY FRAZER, WATKINS, ADAMS & OTHERS;
Upwards of One Hundred Bedsteads and Feather Beds, suitable Mattresses and appropriate Bedding:
WARDROBES AND CHESTS OF DRAWERS,
AND A PROPORTIONATE NUMBER OF DRESSING TABLES AND GLASSES,
And every other Chamber Requisite:
DINING, SOFA, CARD, PEMBROKE AND OCCASIONAL TABLES,
CARPETS AND DRUGGETS,
A Variety of Sofas and Chairs of various Classes: Chintz and Dimity Draperies;
BOOKCASES, CABINETS, WRITING TABLES, GLASS WARE, CHINA;
An extensive Assortment of Copper Appendages for the Kitchen and Confectionary,
TWO WATER CARTS, & MISCELLANEOUS ITEMS OF UTILITY & ORNAMENT.
COMPRISING NEARLY ONE THOUSAND LOTS
Which will be Sold by Auction,
By Mr. PHILLIPS,
ON THE PREMISES,
GLOUCESTER LODGE,
On SATURDAY, 15th of JULY, 1820, and 5 following Days,
(Sunday excepted,) at HALF-PAST ONE o'Clock precisely each Day.

After the King's death in 1820, the Lodge, its contents and adjoining properties in Gloucester Row were sold. It was private residence for some years before its conversion to a hotel in 1859.

The big extension to the south of the hotel dates from 1860 and stands on part of the former royal gardens, as do Royal Terrace and Frederick Place.

The side extension meant a new entrance had to be made in the front of the building.

Disaster on 27th March 1927 when fire destroyed much of the interior.

Post-fire rebuilding added an extra storey to the hotel, a double row of attics in the roof and a verandah.

The verandah was later replaced and in 1988 the former hotel was converted to apartments and its basement area opened up as a pub/restaurant.

Early in 2009 the verandah was removed and both fine Venetian windows can now be seen. The building has reverted to its original name 'Gloucester Lodge'.

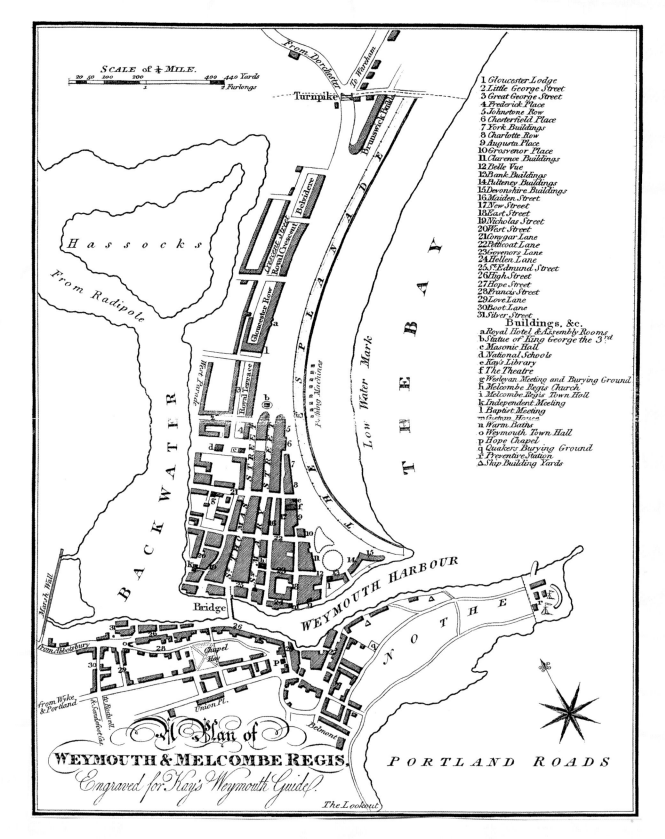

SCALE of ¼ MILE.

20 50 100 200 400 440 Yards

1 Furlong   2 Furlongs

1 Gloucester Lodge
2 Little George Street
3 Great George Street
4 Frederick Place
5 Johnstone Row
6 Chesterfield Place
7 York Buildings
8 Charlotte Row
9 Augusta Place
10 Grosvenor Place
11 Clarence Buildings
12 Belle Vue
13 Bank Buildings
14 Pulteney Buildings
15 Devonshire Buildings
16 Maiden Street
17 New Street
18 East Street
19 Nicholas Street
20 West Street
21 Conygar Lane
22 Petticoat Lane
23 Govenors Lane
24 Hellen Lane
25 St Edmund Street
26 High Street
27 Hope Street
28 Francis Street
29 Love Lane
30 Boot Lane
31 Silver Street

Buildings, &c.
a Royal Hotel & Assembly Rooms
b Statue of King George the 3rd
c Masonic Hall
d National Schools
e Kay's Library
f The Theatre
g Wesleyan Meeting and Burying Ground
h Melcombe Regis Church
i Melcombe Regis Town Hall
k Independent Meeting
l Baptist Meeting
m Gustom House
n Warm Baths
o Weymouth Town Hall
p Hope Chapel
q Quakers Burying Ground
r Preventive Station
△ Ship Building Yards

Turnpike

From Dorchester
To Wareham
Brunswick Buildings

From Radipole

H a s s o c k s

Belvidere

Crescent Street
Royal Crescent

Gloucester Row

THE ESPLANADE

Low Water Mark

THE BAY

Mint Parade

Royal Terrace

B A C K W A T E R

Fishing Machines

Marsh Wall

Bridge

from Abbotsbury

from Wyke & Portland
to Rodwell & Sandsfoot Cas.

Chapel Hay

Union Pl.

WEYMOUTH HARBOUR

Belmont

T H E   N O T H E

P O R T L A N D   R O A D S

A Plan of
WEYMOUTH & MELCOMBE REGIS.
Engraved for Kay's Weymouth Guide.

The Lookout

32

MAP 12

MAP OF WEYMOUTH AND MELCOMBE REGIS

From KAY'S *Weymouth Guide*, 1824

By the time this map appeared in Kay's *Weymouth Guide* of 1824, Weymouth's heyday as the favourite Royal resort had ended, but the results of King George III's patronage can clearly be seen in the expansion of the town and seafront. The King visited Weymouth on fourteen occasions between 1789 and 1805 and other members of the Royal Family holidayed here for some years after that, but Gloucester Lodge (**1** on the map) in Gloucester Row, the house the King had eventually purchased from his brother, William Henry, Duke of Gloucester, was sold in 1820. It was a private residence for some years before conversion to a hotel in the 1850s. By the time Kay's guidebook was published in 1824 much of the former royal gardens had been built on and they were to provide land for Royal Terrace, Frederick Place, Great George Street, Little George Street (later renamed Westham Road), bordered on the west by West Parade (now part of Park Street).

The building boom generated by royal patronage would gradually slow down, but the 1824 map shows many changes since the beginning of the century. A new Town Bridge opened that year – the previous maps of 1774 and 1800 show it crossing the harbour at the end of St Nicholas Street, a site chosen in 1770 but not universally popular. The new bridge reverted to the traditional site at the end of St Thomas Street. There are some developments on the Weymouth side of the harbour with additional buildings being shown in the infilled Hope Square area. The Marsh Wall is named. It appears on earlier maps and town minutes of the early seventeenth century make reference to attempts to stop the tidal waters flooding this low-lying area so it could be used as agricultural land.

The major changes are on Melcombe Regis side and are seaside-holiday related. (Melcombe's 'Regis' has nothing to do with King George III's visits – it dates back to

The new Town Bridge of 1824. An engraving by John Upham, 1825.

An 1834 engraving of The Rings and Devonshire and Pulteney Buildings.

royal ownership in the mediaeval period.) The Esplanade had been extended both to the north and south and Brunswick Buildings (now Brunswick Terrace) at its northern end was completed by 1824. Waterloo Place would follow in the 1830s but heading south, the gap between this terrace and Royal Crescent was not filled until the completion of Belvidere and Victoria Terrace in the 1850s. Kay's map repeats the illusion of a slight curve to Royal Crescent, which is actually a straight row of houses. By this date there are clearly developments behind the Esplanade and West Parade at Park Street's southern end may have been the beginnings of a planned long straight road along the Backwater which later, following further reclamation was to take a different line as Commercial Road.

Coming south along the Esplanade, at '**b**' we find the King's Statue, Weymouth's tribute to King George III and his visits here. The foundation stone was laid with great ceremony on 25th October 1809, as the King entered the 50th year of his reign : the statue was unveiled exactly one year later and stands on a site formerly occupied by a town water supply cistern.

Continuing south, the Esplanade sweeps out in a curve seawards, reclamation begun in 1805 to provide the sites for (**14**) Pulteney and (**15**) Devonshire Buildings. Infill was brought across from the Weymouth side of the harbour where a new boatbuilding yard was under construction and residents were instructed to dump rubbish to build up the area behind the new sea wall here. The triangle and circle of enclosed ground shown was known as 'The Rings' and later became the site of the Alexandra Gardens.

The map indicates a town which was expanding but still within quite a small area: the next decade would see the boundaries extended and plans put forward for a public park on yet more land reclaimed from the Backwater.

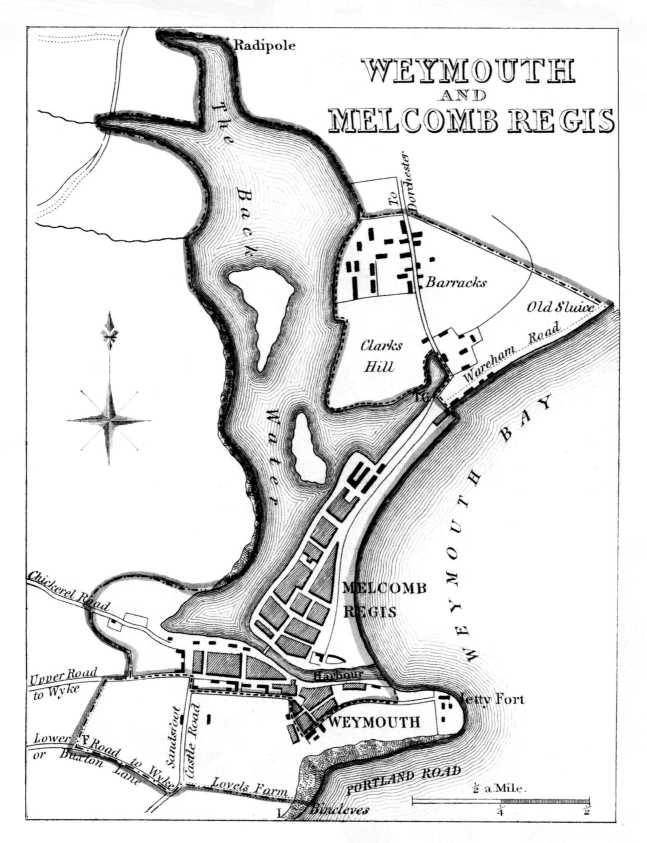

WEYMOUTH
AND
MELCOMB REGIS

Radipole

The Back

Water

Barracks

Old Sluice

To Dorchester

Clarks
Hill

Wareham Road

WEYMOUTH BAY

Chickerel Road

MELCOMB
REGIS

Upper Road
to Wyke

Harbour

Jetty Fort

Lower F Road
or Buxton Lane

Sandsfoot
Castle Road

to Wyke

WEYMOUTH

Lovels Farm

PORTLAND ROAD

Bincleves

½ a Mile.

¼

½

MAP 13

ROBERT CREIGHTON'S MAP OF WEYMOUTH AND MELCOMBE REGIS circa 1832

Drawn by Robert Creighton, this was one of a set of four Dorset maps (the others were of Bridport, Dorchester and Poole) showing the proposed extension of town boundaries under the provisions of the Municipal Corporations Act 1835. The map must be of slightly earlier date as there is no indication of the Park Wall, the foundation stone of which was laid in 1834, part of an ambitious scheme intended to provide a public park on a large area reclaimed from the Backwater.

Although providing very little in the way of town centre detail, the green boundary line shows very clearly that the Borough of Weymouth and Melcombe Regis was contained within quite a small area prior to 1835. In that year the Borough boundary and the Parliamentary boundary became one and the same, as illustrated by the red boundary line.

Note that prior to 1835 most of the Nothe lay outside of the borough and was formerly part of Wyke Regis. Sandsfoot Castle Road on the map is today's Rodwell Road (also known as Longhill Road). Wyke Road was the Upper Road to Wyke and Buxton Road (then Buxton Lane) the Lower Road.

To the north the red line encloses a similar new area to be added to the borough, taking the boundary out to Lodmoor Hill. The Barracks shown are those of the Hanoverian troops of King George III's time and traces of the barrack buildings can still be found off Dorchester Road. On the west side of Dorchester Road, Clark's Hill, also known as Melcombe Common, began to be filled with houses later in the nineteenth century.

Further boundary extensions in the late nineteenth and early twentieth centuries greatly enlarged the borough, bringing in the majority of the villages in the surrounding area. The last major extension occurred in 1974 when Portland became part of the borough. This inclusion of the Island and Royal Manor brought about a change of name, when the former Borough of Weymouth and Melcombe Regis became the Borough of Weymouth and Portland.

Creighton was a well-known cartographer in the early nineteenth century and drew most of the maps (including one of Dorset) for Samuel Lewis's *Topographical Dictionary of England*, first published in 1831.

Left: A contemporary print depicts King George III as 'Brigade Major'.

Radipole Barracks ('The Barracks' on the map) are a reminder of King George III's visits to the town when fears of an attack by the French brought thousands of troops to the area, stationed in local camps and barracks, an influx of soldiers which must have considerably enlivened the rather staid resort. Radipole Terrace at Lodmoor Hill, shown right, is one of the few remaining traces of the barrack buildings at Lodmoor Hill, which were sold off in 1824 when no longer required for defence purposes.

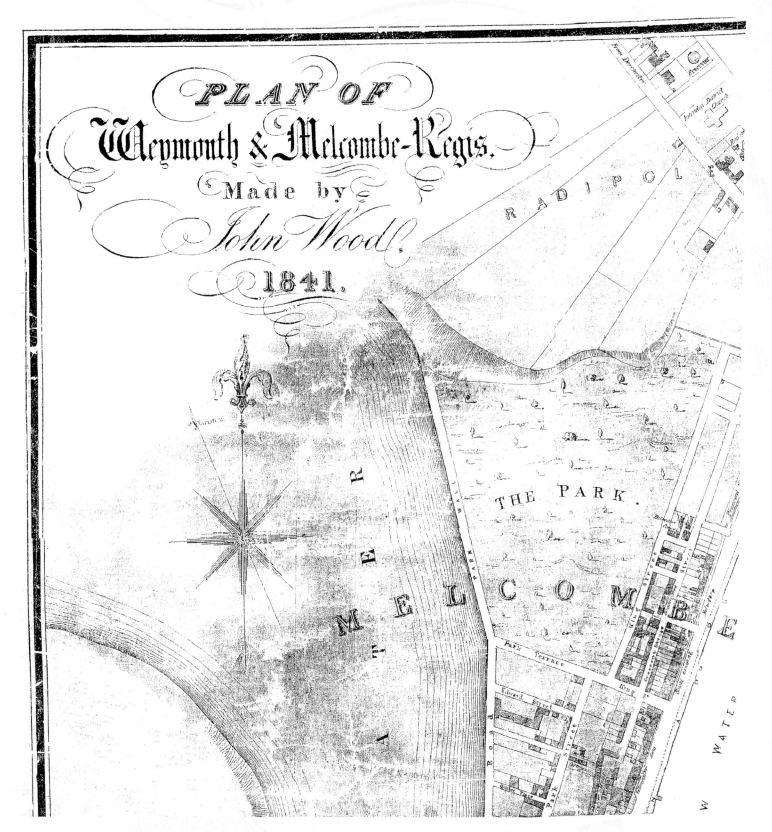

MAP 14

JOHN WOOD'S PLAN OF WEYMOUTH & MELCOMBE REGIS, 1841

In 1841 when John Wood published his plan of the town, there were still hopes that 'The Park', shown on this extract from it, might yet become a reality : it was not to be. Years had passed since plans were put forward for a magnificent public park to be laid out on land reclaimed from The Backwater, north of today's King Street. The Park (following Queen Victoria's accession it was referred to as the Royal Victoria Park) was to have handsome entrance lodges at either end, drives and paths, trees and flowers.

The foundation stone of the retaining wall (Park Wall on the map) had been formally laid with due Civic and Masonic ceremony on 4th June 1834 amidst general celebrations. This was a real gala day when shops and businesses closed, flags flew, crowds turned out and the invited dignitaries, once they had walked in procession to view the proceedings from a spot of high ground near the end of the present Cassiobury Road, returned to the town to enjoy a sumptuous dinner and ball. Even the poor house inhabitants were not forgotten, each being treated to prime roast beef, plum pudding and a pint of strong beer to mark the occasion. Sadly, that one celebratory day could be said to be both the beginning, and the end, of Weymouth's plans for a fine public park.

By the following year things were not going well. The Park Wall was not built high enough and had to be raised to prevent the Backwater from overflowing. Until funds became available to develop the park, the enclosed land was let out for grazing. This was the beginning of sorry saga which eventually allowed the two lessees (one of whom was a former Alderman) who for years had managed to evade all the conditions attached to their lease, to buy the land for a ridiculously low price. Alerted to the sale, a public spirited local townsman brought the 'plot' to the ratepayers' notice, resulting in a successful but costly and lengthy legal action which raised the sale price of the land from £162.15s to almost £5000.

All hopes of a park were then abandoned. The Great Western and South Western railway companies planned to bring their lines into the town and the park area was the ideal location. A slice of the reclaimed land was purchased for lines and station buildings, the railway eventually opening in January 1857. The Conservative Land Society bought the rest for housing and Park Street today leads not to one of those planned park entrance lodges but to the terraced streets which still bear the name 'Park District'.

As can be seen on the map, building along the Esplanade had slowed somewhat since the days of King George III and 'Royal Weymouth'. Belvidere was not completed and work had not begun on Victoria Terrace.

Some street names have changed: Park Terrace became part of the present King Street and the King Street shown here running parallel to the Esplanade was renamed Queen Street in 1872.

AT A

MEETING

Of the Inhabitants appointed to be held this day at the Guild-Hall, pursuant to a request to the Mayor, for taking into consideration the best means of celebrating the Day appointed for the commencement of the

IMPROVEMENTS

IN THE

BACK WATER

The following Resolutions were unanimously adopted :—

GEORGE ARDEN, Esq. Mayor,

(By Desire,) IN THE CHAIR.

1st.—SIR HUNGERFORD HOSKINS, Bart., moved and the same was seconded by J. W. WESTON, Esq. M.C.

That the Corporation by their contemplated Improvements in inclosing a part of the Back Water, and forming a Park at the entrance of the Town, are entitled to the Best Thanks of the Inhabitants ; and that this Meeting do offer them their cordial acknowledgments for the same, and pledge themselves to render every assistance in their power to forward so laudable an undertaking.

2nd.—Moved by WM. WHARTON BURDON, Esq., seconded by AMBROSE LARKWORTHY, Jun. Esq.,

That an Improvement of such magnitude in this town ought, in the opinion of this Meeting, to be commenced with every demonstration of public approbation and rejoicing ; and in order to give eclat, the Corporation are requested to attend in their official capacity, and call to their assistance the Masonic and other Societies, to lay the Foundation Stone in Form.

3rd.—Moved by JOHN HENNING, Esq., Seconded by Mr. THOMAS,

That a Committee of Five Persons be named for the purpose of making the necessary arrangements, with power to add to their numbers.

4th.—Moved by LIEUT. SCRIVEN, R.N., Seconded by Mr. ROBINSON,

That a Subscription be entered into to defray the expenses attendant on laying the Foundation Stone.

5th.—Moved by Mr. LARKWORTHY, Seconded by LIEUT. SCRIVEN, R.N.

That the 4th of JUNE be the day for laying the Foundation Stone.

6th.—Moved by Mr. W. J. HILL, Seconded by Mr. JAMES MILLEDGE,

That these Resolutions be printed and advertized in the *Dorset County Chronicle and Somersetshire Gazette.*

GEORGE ARDEN, Chairman.

7th.—Moved by SIR HUNGERFORD, HOSKINS, Bart., Seconded by WILLIAM WHARTON, BURDON, Esq.

That the Cordial Thanks of this Meeting be given to the Mayor, for his able conduct in the Chair, and his readiness at all times to meet the wishes of the Inhabitants.

Weymouth, 14th May, 1834.

BENSON, Letter-press and Copper-plate Printer, WEYMOUTH.

A promising start for the proposed park.

A day of great celebration as the foundation stone of the Park Wall is laid on 4th June 1834.

The high land where the crowd watched a waterborne gun fire a triumphal salute in 1834 is in the background of this picture. More reclamation followed in the twentieth century.

Today the railway land in the previous picture is now the site of the Jubilee Business Park and its shops.

WEYMOUTH.

Proposals for making Pleasure Grounds with appropriate Walks and Drives at the Royal Victoria Park near the Belvidere.

It has long been a subject of regret, amongst Persons interested in the prosperity of this Town, that Weymouth, with a Bay unequalled for its beauty and with every desirable Marine convenience and advantage, should be deficient in Walks and Drives. And it cannot be doubted, but that Pleasure Grounds possessing these advantages, will greatly add to the attractions which for many Years have rendered this place so favorite a Fashionable Resort, and make it the most complete and delightful Watering Place in the Kingdom.

With these views it is proposed to form a Company, for converting about Twenty Five Acres of Ground near the Belvidere, of which a Lease was granted by the late Corporation for an absolute Term of 75 Years, into Pleasure Grounds, to be called "THE ROYAL VICTORIA PARK." And it is believed that the Subscribers may calculate on a good return of Interest for the Capital expended on the following principles;—

1st. That there shall be a paid-up Capital of £2,500.

2nd. That the Capital shall be raised in 500 Shares of £5 each.

3rd. That as soon as the Subscription List is full, a General Meeting of the Subscribers shall be called for the purpose of appointing Directors and other Officers, and making such Rules and Regulations as may be deemed necessary for carrying the intended plan into effect.

The following Gentlemen have consented to form a Provisional Committee, Viz.

G. C. WELSFORD, Esq. (Mayor)
WILLIAM DEVENISH, Esq.
WILLIAM ELIOT, Esq.
Mr. TASKER.
Mr. JOHN HANCOCK.

And applications for Shares to be directed (post paid) to Mr. GEORGE ARDEN, SOLICITOR, WEYMOUTH.

Weymouth, 5th November, 1838.

THOMAS, PRINTER, ROYAL LIBRARY, WEYMOUTH.

Weymouth.

SALE OF VICTORIA PARK!

The Town Council having at a Meeting held at the Council Chamber on Thursday the 16th instant, Resolved and Ordered that the Reversion in fee of the intended

NEW PARK,

acquired by the late Corporation at a cost of Fifteen Hundred Pounds, be offered to the Lessees, Messrs. Charles B. Fooks and William Lock, for the sum of ONE HUNDRED AND SIXTY TWO POUNDS, whereby (should the sale be effected) the Inhabitants will be deprived of the only remaining portion of Land within the Town capable of being formed into Public Walks and Drives, so much required for the health and amusement of the rapidly increasing population and visitors.

WE, the undersigned, beg to announce that a Meeting of the INHABITANTS and RESIDENT VISITORS will be held at the Royal-Hotel, on Wednesday the 22nd instant, at 12 o'clock, to take the same into consideration, and to adopt measures for preventing the completion of the sale, and to secure to the Inhabitants the object originally intended by the Corporation.

T. P. Howard	Benjamin Benson
J. C. Hawkins	Thomas Kent
W. L. G. Thomas	Henry Harris
Richard Bower	John Jenkins Rolls
J. Mortimer	Joseph Ayling
R. T. Hancock	Robert Dominy
John Henning	John Judd
William Hodges	A. S. Tucker
George Andrews	G. M. Bidwell
M. Vertue	Thomas Barling
J. E. Ward	Philip Dodson
T. D. Bayly	Daniel Pidgeon
Thomas B. Trowbridge	George P. Scott
Thomas Atherton	R. Cotterell
George Welsford	Thomas Dodson
George Kay	Richard Groves
Joseph Tasker	James Eaton Robens
J. Flower	

FEBRUARY 20, 1843.

Printed by G. KAY, Stationer &c., No. 1, St. Mary-Street, Weymouth.

The plans…

…and the scandal over the sale of the proposed park land.

(Bottom, right) If the Southampton and Dorchester Railway proposals of 1844 had been followed through, Weymouth might have had neither Park nor Park District. The Company considered bringing an additional line into the town from near Moreton, through Poxwell, Osmington and Preston, to end up in a second railway station behind the seafront (in the region of Victoria Terrace) with an additional line to the present station site which would have curved round in a big loop where the Park District houses now stand. Like many proposals of the Railway Mania age, this plan failed to materialise. (The terrace shown at the bottom of the plan is Waterloo Place.)

Not a park, but 'Western Walk' was laid out as a path along the 'Park Wall'. It disappeared under later reclamation, but today the town does have 'Radipole Park Gardens' along the lakeside which followed in the wake of 1920s' and 1930s' infilling.

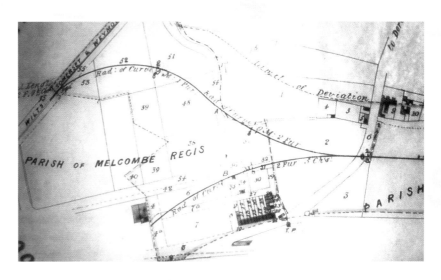

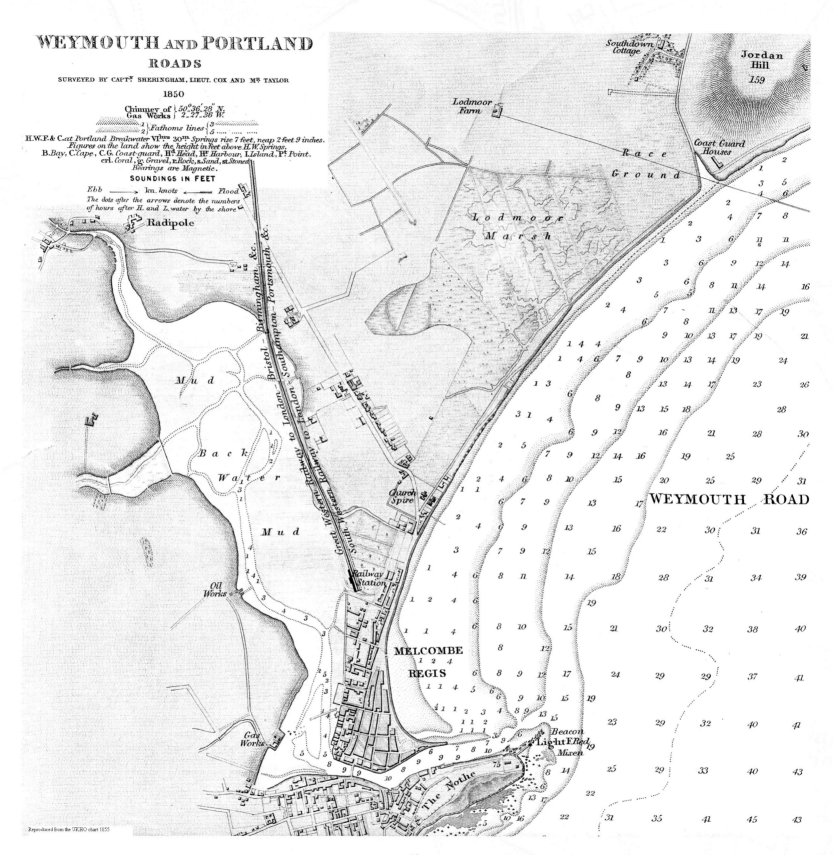

WEYMOUTH AND PORTLAND
ROADS

SURVEYED BY CAPT.ᴺ SHERINGHAM, LIEUT. COX AND M.ᴿ TAYLOR

1850

Chimney of } 50°.36′.28″ N.
Gas Works } 2.27.36 W.
Fathoms lines {1 3
{2 5
H.W.F. & C. at Portland Breakwater VI.ʰʳˢ 30ᵐ Springs rise 7 feet, neap 2 feet 9 inches.
Figures on the land show the height in feet above H.W. Springs.
B. Bay, C. Cape, C.G. Coast-guard, H.ᵈ Head, H.ʳ Harbour, I. Island, P.ᵗ Point.
crl. Coral, g. Gravel, r. Rock, s. Sand, st. Stones.
Bearings are Magnetic.
SOUNDINGS IN FEET

Ebb ——→   kn. knots   ←—— Flood
The dots after the arrows denote the numbers
of hours after H. and L. water by the shore

Radipole

Lodmoor
Farm

Southdown
Cottage

Jordan
Hill
159

Coast Guard
Houses

Race

Ground

Lodmoor
Marsh

Mud

Back

Water

Mud

Oil
Works

Railway
Station

WEYMOUTH   ROAD

Church
Spire

MELCOMBE

REGIS

Gas
Works

Beacon
Light F Red
Mixed

The Nothe

MAP 15

CHART OF WEYMOUTH AND PORTLAND ROADS

Published by the Admiralty Hydrographic Office, 1855

This is the Weymouth section of the local Admiralty chart of 1850. It was actually published by the Admiralty Hydrographic Office in 1855 and incorporates some post-1850 developments, namely the lines of the Great Western and South Western dual-gauge railway (although the railway to Weymouth did not actually open until January 1857) and the 'Church Spire' of St John's church, consecrated in 1854.

Obviously maritime features predominate, but as the map is finely engraved, many of the town details are also of interest. To the north, below Jordan Hill, can be seen the Coastguard Cottages several of which have fallen into the sea over the years due to coastal erosion at this spot. Horse races were held at the nearby Race Ground north of Lodmoor from 1821 until the early 1880s. Lodmoor Farm is more usually known as Southdown Farm.

The River Wey meanders down to the harbour mouth via the mud flats of the Backwater – tidal in those days and often decidedly smelly. The 'night soil' collected in carts from the privies and cesspits of the town's houses was usually dumped in the Backwater, which thus acted as the town sewer. At low tide the sights and odours from a combination of stagnant water and human excrement were a source of constant complaint in the Victorian period, although little was done to solve the problem until the very end of the nineteenth century.

The term 'Radipole Lake' for the upper reaches of the Backwater seems to have been adopted as a more picturesque term for the waters above Westham Bridge in the 1920s. There was no road bridge to Westham in 1855 (the first was opened in 1859) and little reason to cross to the fields on the far shore as two industrial sites were all that stood there – Braithwaite and Co's Oil and Spirit Works and the town Gas Works. The tall chimney of the Gas Works was an important sea mark, its position noted at the top of the chart.

Of those who carried out the 1850 survey, the best known was probably Captain William Sheringham who worked in the Admiralty's hydrography department from the 1830s until 1853. He was already familiar with the area, having been requested by the Hydrographer of the Navy, Sir Francis Beaufort, to give his opinion on the location of a proposed breakwater at Portland. Sheringham arrived aboard HMS *Fearless* in May 1844 and his report was much in favour of the enclosure of Portland Roads, appreciating also the comparatively low cost of materials if thousands of tons of waste stone from the island quarries were used in the construction. (*See also* MAPS 43 – 48)

Horseracing at Lodmoor in the mid-nineteenth century.

St John's church spire, still a striking landmark, seen here in the snowy winter of 2010.

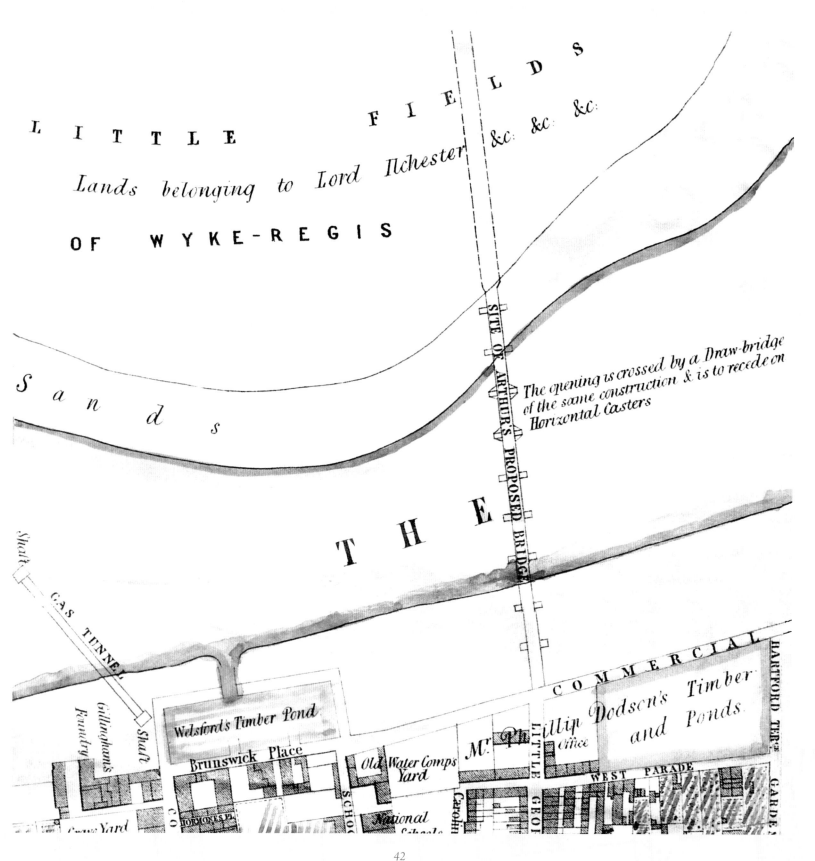

LITTLE FIELDS

Lands belonging to Lord Ilchester &c: &c: &c:

OF WYKE-REGIS

Sands

SITE OF ARTHUR'S PROPOSED BRIDGE

The opening is crossed by a Draw-bridge
of the same construction & is to recede on
Horizontal Casters

THE

Shaft

GAS TUNNEL

Gillingham's Foundry

Shaft

Welsford's Timber Pond

Brunswick Place

Old Water Comps Yard

COMMERCIAL

Mr Phillip Dodson's Timber and Ponds

Office

LITTLE GEO

HARTFORD TERᶜᵉ

Caroline

WEST PARADE

GARDENS

Crows Yard

HORLOCKES Pᵗ

SCHOOL

National Schools

MAP 16

PIERSE ARTHUR'S TRIGONOMETRICAL MAP OF WEYMOUTH, 1857

The 1850s saw proposals for crossing the Backwater by way of a timber bridge from the end of Little George Street (today's Westham Road) to Westham, a then undeveloped area known as Littlefields, but destined to become a suburb of high density housing by the end of the nineteenth century.

Arthur's Backwater Bridge of 1859, with the long drawbridge he specified.

The designer of the first Backwater Bridge was Pierse Arthur and in 1857 he published the first of his 'Trigonometrical Maps' of Weymouth, showing his plan for the bridge. The large coloured map measures around 4 feet by 2½ feet (122 cm x 76 cm) and the scale is approximately 25" = 1 mile (1:2500). It is a superb plan of the town and the extracts on the following pages are taken from the original and also from slightly later editions of smaller scale.

The Backwater Bridge after the removal of the drawbridge in the 1880s.

Arthur's appearance in Weymouth is something of a mystery. He was born in Ireland and appears only in one local Census Return, that of 1851, when he was living on Portland. His occupation is listed as 'Civil Engineer' so he may possibly have had some connection with the breakwater works then in progress.

His map of Weymouth is delightfully idiosyncratic, bearing as it does his forthright opinions on local building projects – 'ill erected' was his comment on the recently extended pier and although his plan shows the town's new railway lines and station (opened in 1857) he added a note 'Wilts and Somerset Railway 11 years in hand & not yet completed!!!'

Pierse Arthur's bridge was replaced by the present Westham Bridge in 1921, with a footbridge added in 1973-74. The bridge has carried no traffic since the installation of a new road system in 1987 and is now used for car parking and a Sunday Farmers' Market.

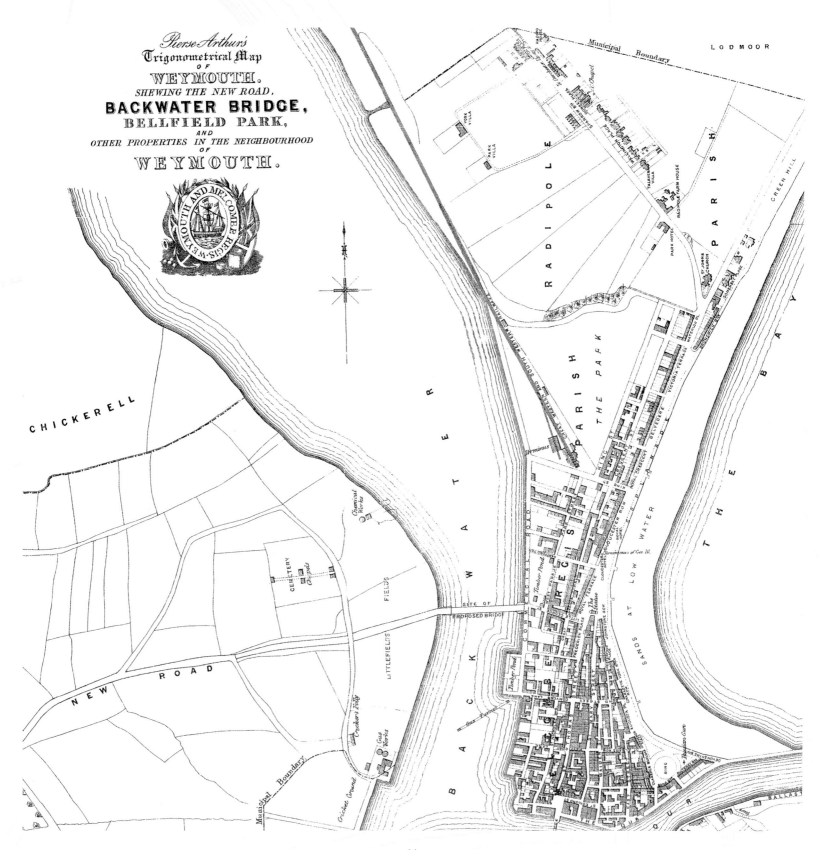

Pierse Arthur's
Trigonometrical Map
OF
WEYMOUTH.
SHEWING THE NEW ROAD,
BACKWATER BRIDGE,
BELLFIELD PARK,
AND
OTHER PROPERTIES IN THE NEIGHBOURHOOD
OF
WEYMOUTH.

MAP 17

PIERSE ARTHUR'S TRIGONOMETRICAL MAP OF WEYMOUTH, 1857

This extract is from one of Pierse Arthur's smaller-scale maps of the late 1850s. The proposed Backwater Bridge he designed opened in 1859 and the 'New Road' shown leading westwards from it is today's Abbotsbury Road. For some local residents, their first trip across the bridge was possibly also their last, as a new Melcombe Regis Cemetery opened here in 1856, after overcrowding of the town centre cemeteries had become a serious health problem. The Chemical Works nearby were a short-lived attempt to produce oil from Purbeck shale but they later reverted their original use as a pottery. Barges requiring access to the works were one of the reasons for the inclusion of a drawbridge in the first Backwater Bridge, and it was also hoped that the Great Western Railway might make use of land near the railway station on the opposite shore for port development. This was not proceeded with and the drawbridge was eventually considered to be redundant. It was removed in the 1880s following the building of a dam just south of it which would have been a serious inconvenience for boat traffic.

The railway to Weymouth opened on 20th January 1857 and although Arthur names the triangle of land alongside the terminus as 'The Park', in reality plans to lay out a public park on this land reclaimed from the Backwater in 1834 had ended long ago. The scandal over its cut-price sale to members of the council, a lengthy court case and the coming of the railway led to protests then eventual apathy over the proposed 'Royal Victoria Park'. The remaining land was sold to the Conservative Land Society which filled the area with the streets of terraced houses which are known today as the 'Park District' and bear the names of nineteenth century Tory politicians.

To the north, and inside the extended borough boundary of 1835, can be seen the former barrack square of the Georgian Radipole Barracks, which had housed Hanoverian troops in the days of King George III's visits to Weymouth. York Villa was part of the barrack buildings as was Park Villa (since demolished). The barracks were sold off in the 1820s when no longer required for military use. (Compare with MAP 20, the 6" = 1 mile Ordnance Survey map of 1864)

The view across the Backwater to 'Littlefields Fields' in 2011. Twentieth century reclamation had brought more industrial use of this site (an enlarged gas works, electricity generating station, council depot ; see MAPS 37 and 38) but this has now largely been replaced by housing and office premises, apart from one large 1957 gasholder, now used for gas storage.

MAP 18

PIERSE ARTHUR'S TRIGONOMETRICAL MAP OF WEYMOUTH, 1857

A second extract from Pierse Arthur's smaller-scale map of the late-1850s shows the extensive area once occupied by Belfield House and its grounds. The parklands of this fine mansion, thought to have been designed for the Buxton family by John Crunden and built circa 1780, once extended as far as Cross Road and two driveways led to the house from Wyke Road and Buxton Road. Some of its stabling and farm buildings shown here still stand along Buxton Road.

Belfield House has recently undergone a fine and sympathetic restoration but its park is no more. In the 1860s the rector of St Mary's church, Melcombe Regis was the wealthy Reverend Talbot Greaves. Although the church provided him with a fine residence in St Thomas Street (the present No. 82, currently part of The Clipper pub), Greaves preferred to live out of town and purchased part of Belfield's grounds, on which he built a large house known as 'Portmore'. After he left the area, his house was converted to a private school and renamed 'Connaught House', later becoming council-owned and providing temporary post-Second World War accommodation for local schoolchildren. Today, Connaught House has gone – demolished in 1988 – and its site is now filled with houses. Some of its grounds provided a site in the 1950s for Holy Trinity Infants and Junior Schools which were replaced here by a new building in 2007.

More of Belfield's park disappeared in the 1930s when the then owner sold much of the land around the house. On the map, the drive shown passing close to the front of Belfield House became Belfield Park Avenue, with houses on both sides along its length and a little later Belfield Park Close filled more of the house's former grounds.

The map also shows Smallmouth Sands and the note 'From Portland, via Sands' indicates that this was formerly the route of the Turnpike Trust road, which led from today's Old Castle Road along the shore to Smallmouth (Ferrybridge).

Three early views of Belfield House and its park. John Love's view of 1790 (in the oval frame) and two engravings of watercolours by John Upham just a few years later.

Belfield House in 2011.

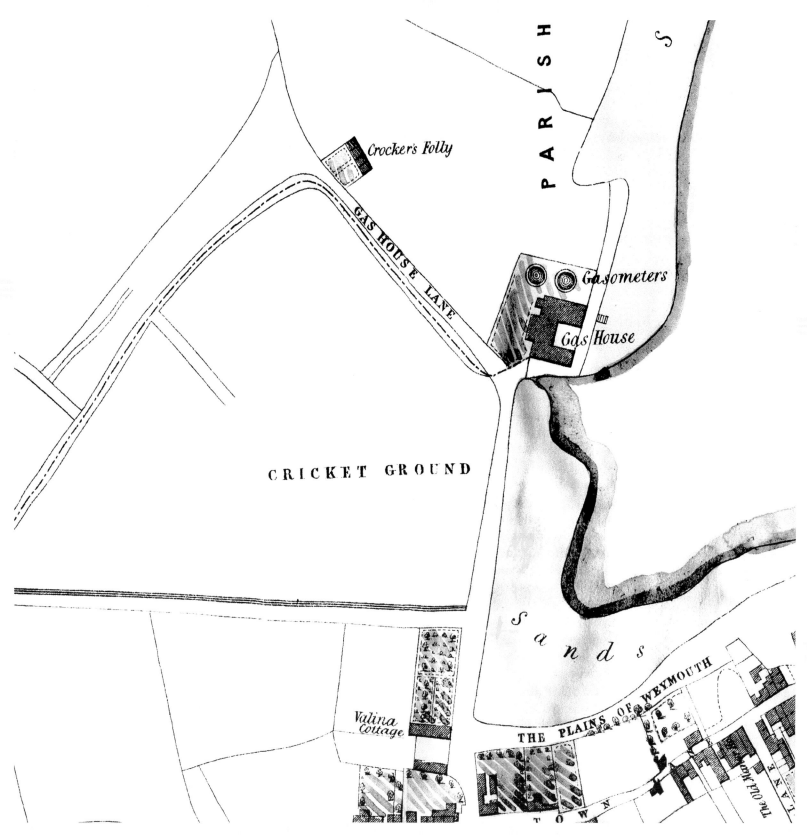

MAP 19

PIERSE ARTHUR'S TRIGONOMETRICAL MAP OF WEYMOUTH, 1857

A final section from one of Pierse Arthur's 1850s' maps shows the 'Sands' where today the Asda supermarket stands, linking North Quay and 'The Plains of Weymouth' with Westwey Road, which was not completed until 1930, prior to which the western shore of the Backwater, as shown here, was merely a sandy strip.

Reclamation of the Marsh area, initially by building a wall to keep the tidal waters out, led to the establishment of the Victorian cricket ground, land later crossed by the embankment of the Weymouth and Portland Railway. The Sidney Hall, another of Weymouth's lost buildings, opened in 1900 and lasted until 1987, when it and the adjacent Weymouth Football Ground made way for the present supermarket and its car parks.

Two buildings not many yards apart in distance but several centuries difference in time. Netherton House close to the foot of Boot Hill is the 'The Old Manor House' on the map. Asda supermarket, its car parks and an apartment block filled the site of Weymouth Football Ground and Sidney Hall.

Town Lane at the base of the map is today's Chickerell Road, and the Old Manor House (Netherton House) stands at its junction with Boot Lane (now Boot Hill, or, more correctly, Rodwell Road).

Newcastle colliery owner William Burdon's not altogether satisfactory gas works opened in 1836 and were purchased by the local council in 1867, following many complaints about the inefficient and unreliable gas supply to the town. Gas House Lane (now Newstead Road) led towards Crocker's Folly, since demolished. The origin of its name is unknown, unless it was thought unwise to own a property so close to the malodorous gas works. Nothing of these gas works buildings remains today and Westwey House occupies their site : the present gasholder on Westwey Road is of much later date, erected in the 1950s and still used for gas storage. The council ownership of the gas works ceased with nationalisation in 1948 and gas production in Weymouth ceased altogether in 1958.

The Sidney Hall of 1900, a gift to Holy Trinity parish in memory of his son Sidney by Sir John Groves of the brewery. Demolished in 1987.

Reclamation from the Backwater (or Inner Harbour) in the late 1920s provided a new harbour wall behind which Westwey Road was laid out and opened in 1930, with extensions to the gas works being completed in 1933.

The foundation stone and coat of arms from the Sidney Hall can be seen in the supermarket car park.

(See also MAPS 37, 38 and 65 for later developments along Westwey Road)

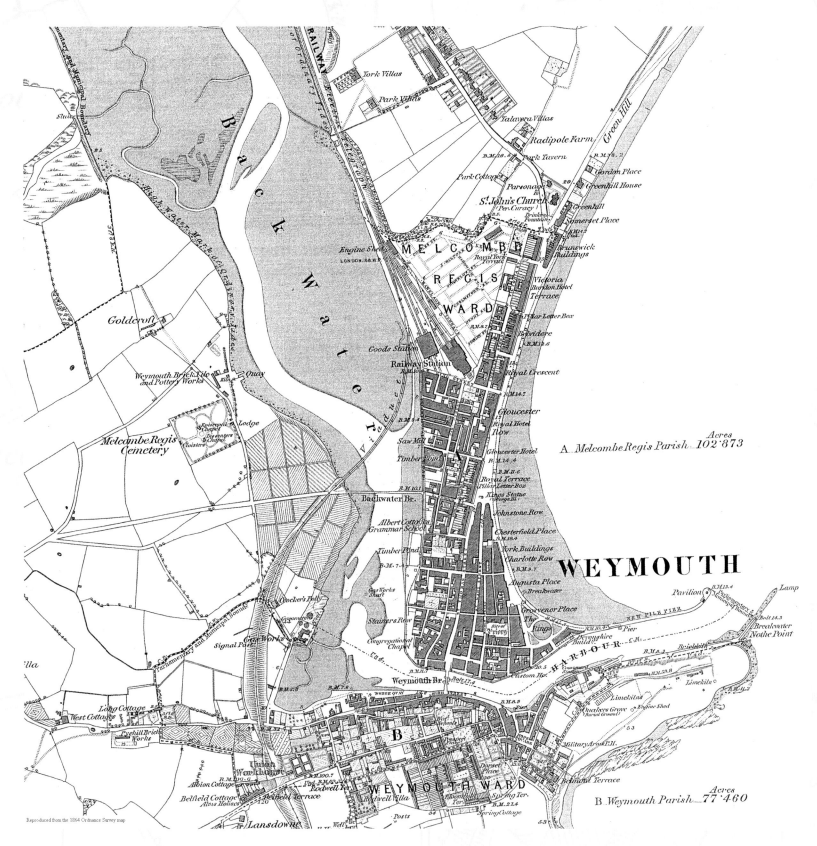

MAP 20

ORDNANCE SURVEY 1864 (Scale 6″ = 1 mile) WEYMOUTH

The years 1863-4 saw publication of the first of the larger-scale Dorset Ordnance Survey maps and this extract is of Weymouth at a scale of 6″ = 1 mile (1 : 10,560). Also published at that time were the large scale maps of Weymouth and the surrounding area at a scale of 25″ = 1 mile (1 : 2500) and even more detailed maps of the town centre at a scale of 10.56 feet = 1 mile (1 : 500). Although some in the series appeared in 1863, these maps are generally known as the '1864 Ordnance Survey'.

This 6″ map indicates considerable changes in the town since the publication of Pierse Arthur's map of only six years earlier (*see* MAP 17). All thoughts of a public park having been abandoned, it shows a plan of the streets which were to fill the reclaimed triangle of land at the northern end of the town between the railway and the Esplanade.

As well as the 1859 Backwater Bridge for road traffic, a second bridge had been built across the water to carry the line of the Weymouth and Portland Railway (opened in 1865). There were now development plans for the open fields on the Backwater's western shore, already bisected by the railway line and a grid plan shows proposed roads branching off Abbotsbury Road. Goldcroft Farm was probably newly-established when the map was published. The Weymouth and Portland Railway closed in 1965 and the rail bridge and its successor are long gone, but it is still possible to follow the old track, now tarmac-ed and known as the Rodwell Trail, from Westham to Ferrybridge at Wyke Regis, where another bridge once took the trains across to Portland.

Much of what is shown here remains today, but some buildings in the town centre are long gone. Albert Cottages stood in Lower Park Street on what is now the back of Wilkinsons store; a grammar school occupied the present Sure Start building in Commercial Road, probably best remembered in recent years as the Arts Centre; heading down towards the Town Bridge, the 1804 Congregational chapel's later occupants included a theatre, a foundry and a cold store before the building's demolition and replacement in the 1990s by the present flats at the end of West Street.

Formerly a Victorian school building, from the 1950s until it closed in 2008 this was Weymouth and South Dorset Arts Centre.

Altered in 2004, the building in Commercial Road is now home to the Sure Start centre and Weymouth College's exhibition area.

MAP 21

ORDNANCE SURVEY 1864 (Scale 25″= 1 mile) WEYMOUTH : Town Centre

This map, and the six which follow, are reproduced from the 25″ = 1 mile Weymouth maps of 1863-4. Despite being almost 150 years old, the originals have a colour and vibrancy undimmed by time and are a delight to use. Some sheets were updated in 1869 with the addition of new railways and a number were reprinted in 1882.

On this town centre map it is possible to follow the 1865 Weymouth Harbour Tramway railway line right around the town. There are changed street names (Petticoat Lane is now St Alban Street) and lost street names (Bury Street), many public houses long gone (the Fox, the Bear, the Three Tuns etc.), some large town centre private gardens – and no gardens at all at the southern end of the Esplanade where 'The Rings' stood on reclaimed ground which would later become the Alexandra Gardens. The Breakwater shown nearby was an early nineteenth century attempt to stop frequent wave damage at this end of the Esplanade in rough weather. When first built it was longer and higher, but it is now partially lost under later extensions to the prom, although a section of its stone base still lies buried below the sands.

The mediaeval Priory (or Friary) site, once far larger, had been much built over by the 1860s. In pre-Reformation days this had been the Dominican Friary of Melcombe Regis, founded in 1418. The last trace of it – an old doorway in Governor's Lane – was removed in the 1960s.

The remains of the Esplanade breakwater in the early 1900s.

Last fragment of the old Friary – this doorway in Governor's Lane.

All the buildings shown in the picture on the left were removed in the 1950s and 1960s to make way for the car park in East Street.

MELCO

MAP 22

ORDNANCE SURVEY 1864 (Scale 25″ = 1 mile) WEYMOUTH : School Street to King Street

Another section of the 1864/1883 25-inch Ordnance Survey map of the town centre, heads north, from School Street to King Street, with the Weymouth railway station just visible top centre.

Little George Street, later renamed Westham Road, led to the first wooden Backwater Bridge of 1859 (replaced by the present Westham Bridge in 1921). Philip Dodson, thrice Mayor of Weymouth in the Victorian period, built the first Backwater Bridge and close by were the timber yard and timber pond he once owned, today the site of Park Street car park.

The houses of Commercial Road in the 1860s directly overlooked the Backwater, a scene which reclamation was to change greatly in the early twentieth century. A site immediately south of the bridge was infilled to provide a site for Melcombe Regis School of 1912, a primary school which took the same name as an earlier private school nearby. North of the bridge massive reclamation in the 1920s provided ground for Melcombe Regis Gardens, a bowling green and tennis courts. The lines of the Weymouth Harbour Tramway along Commercial Road (still in place, although disused today) are shown and those of the Weymouth and Portland Railway can be seen heading off across the Backwater via a wooden viaduct to Littlfields at Westham.

On the seafront the old bow-fronted Royal Hotel shown was replaced by the present building in the late 1890s. The Gloucester Hotel, formerly King George III's holiday home, was converted to a hotel in the 1850s, its once fine gardens having provided the sites for Royal Terrace and Frederick Place.

On the sands a little symbol denotes 'Post Pipe to Baths' – from here sea water was pumped to the 'Royal Baths' at the top end of the main streets. No royal connections here, for the baths opened in 1842 long after George III's visits ended. They provided hot and cold sea water baths for those who preferred not to venture into the open waters of the Bay.

(Compare this map with MAP 67, the same area in the 1950s)

'Stacie's' opened in 1773 and became the first Royal Hotel, replaced by …

… today's Royal Hotel, opened in 1899.

The Royal Baths of 1842…

…and the building which replaced them in 1927.

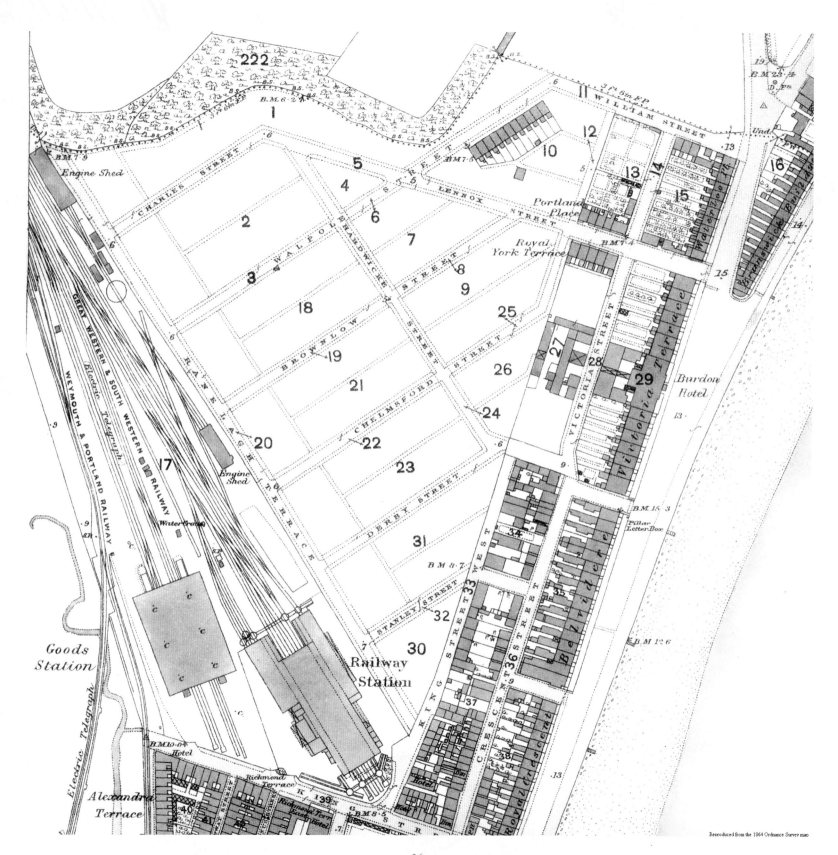

Reproduced from the 1864 Ordnance Survey map

MAP 23

ORDNANCE SURVEY 1864 (Scale 25"= 1 mile)
WEYMOUTH : Railway Station and Park District

Moving north again, the 1860s map shows the area originally intended to be laid out as a public park (*compare with* MAP 14, *John Wood's map of 1841*) but by this date occupied by the lines and station buildings of the Great Western and the London and South Western Railway companies, the main line being dual gauge until 1874. Heading off across the Backwater is the Weymouth and Portland Railway and also shown is the start of the Weymouth Harbour Tramway, branching off along Commercial Road, both these lines opening in 1865. The tramway was horse-drawn in its early years, locos taking over around 1880, and was a goods-only service until 1889 when the line began carrying passengers to and from the Great Western steamers at the Pier.

The remainder of the triangle of reclaimed land was sold to the Conservative Land Society in 1858, a year after the railway opened. The Society was an early form of building society, buying up land in various parts of the country and laying out estates on which it offered freehold plots for sale. Legal fees and mortgages were advanced by the Society, to be repaid at moderate rates of interest. With 300 plots on offer in Weymouth's Park District, the Society hoped to reap its reward with a goodly number of Tory votes from those householders who would not otherwise have been able to afford homes of their own.

The plans shows the proposed street layout, although only one terrace of houses in Walpole Street had been completed by this date. The Society specified the value of the houses to be built in each street – for example, those in Ranelagh Road (Ranelagh Terrace on the map) were to cost £400 – these were the most expensive, others being priced at £180, £140 going down to a more affordable £50 3s 0d. The choice of Ranelagh Road as the best site is a little odd – it may have been useful to live so close to the railway station but it wasn't long before there were complaints about smoke, noise and shrill whistles. House building progress was fairly slow and tended to be piecemeal construction of small terraces. For this reason street-numbering was not introduced until much later and today's family history researchers attempting to identify an ancestor's address by a long-lost terrace name can be faced with quite a task.

Although it seemed at the time that housing was the solution to the Park problem, the Conservative Land Society failed to carry out proper drainage of the estate, which lies below sea level. Heavy rain almost inevitably resulted in flooding and it was well into the twentieth century before the this recurring nuisance was properly tackled.

Street names are those of Victorian Tory politicians. Viscount Ranelagh was Chairman of the Conservative Land Society, another official was Colonel Brownlow Knox. Lord Derby was three-times Prime Minister,

Spencer Horatio Walpole was another leading Tory. Hardwick Street, named after Tory MP the 4th Earl Hardwicke, has for some reason lost the final 'e' of its name over time.

Penny Street is not shown on the map. It must have been an afterthought by the planners as it runs between Charles Street and Walpole Street and occupies what was intended to be one of the 'lanes' which run behind the Park District houses, and hence has no exit onto Ranelagh Road.

Edwardian visitors at Weymouth's original railway station – the line opened on 20th January 1857. (*See also* MAPS 71 *and* 72)

In Walpole Street, this was the first terrace to be built in the Park District

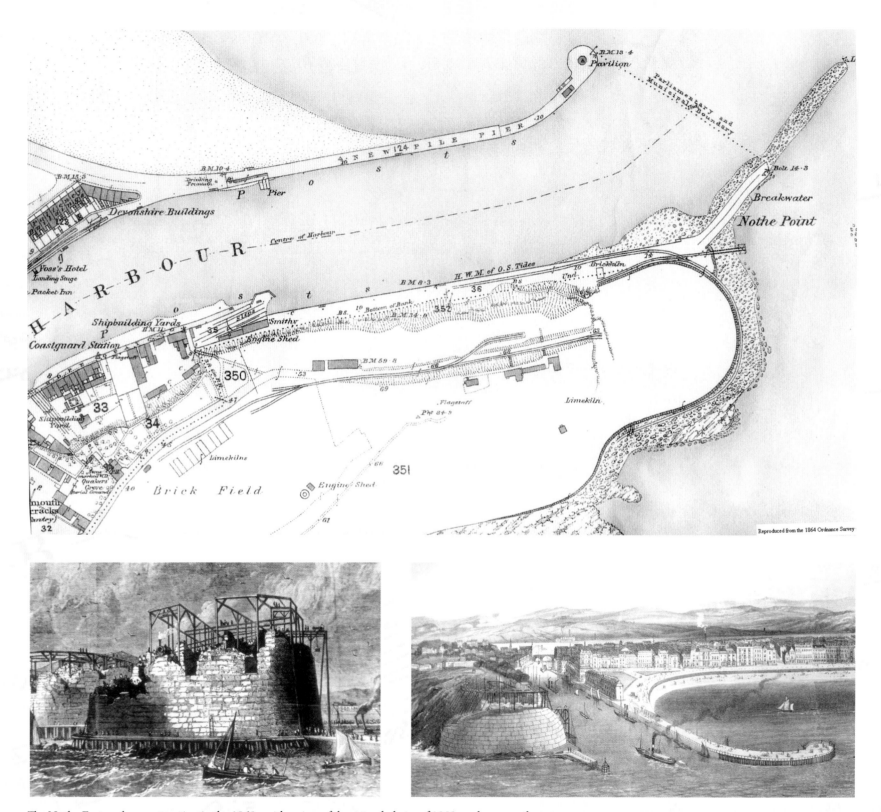

The Nothe Fort under construction in the 1860s, with a view of the extended pier of 1859, as shown on the map.

MAP 24

ORDNANCE SURVEY 1864 (Scale 25 ″= 1 mile)
WEYMOUTH : Harbour, Pier and Nothe

The Outer Harbour, another extract from the 1863/4 Ordnance Survey 25″ maps, showing Pulteney and Devonshire Buildings and the newly extended pile pier of 1859.

Across the harbour on the Weymouth side, the map shows some of the works in connection with the construction of the Nothe Fort, work on which began in 1860. This was part of the impressive Portland Breakwaters defence scheme commenced in 1849, which included the Verne Citadel and other local coastal fortifications. From the 1870s onwards details of barracks, defence works and prisons were omitted from Ordnance Survey large-scale maps and this may be why little of the construction of the Nothe Fort itself is shown on this edition, reprinted in 1882.

The shipbuilding yards along Nothe Parade belonged at this date to the local firms Ayles and Besant. Ayles yard with its picturesque eighteenth century slipmaster's house, is now known as Nelson's Wharf.

Pulteney and Devonshire Buildings in 1826 and 2011, with contrasting shipping in the harbour.

Ayles shipyard in 1844 (with the racing yacht *Conquest* on the stocks) and 2011.

Reproduced from the 1864 Ordnance Survey map

MAP 25

ORDNANCE SURVEY 1864 (Scale 25″= 1 mile) WEYMOUTH : Hope Square

Another of the 25″= 1 mile Weymouth town maps of 1864, of the Hope Square area on the southern side of the harbour, where the open spaces of the Victorian period shown here were to be filled with houses in the latter half of the twentieth century.

Around Hope Square (top right) the brewery buildings of Weymouth Brewery and Hope Brewery, already extensive, would be enlarged in the early years of the twentieth century. It was here that John Groves built his tall-chimneyed red brick building in 1904, next door to rival brewer Devenish. The two breweries amalgamated in 1960 and under the Devenish name traded until the 1980s, when brewing transferred to Cornwall. The empty buildings were remodelled, opening in 1989 as 'Brewer's Quay', a mix of shopping village, Museum and Timewalk

(a sights and sounds journey through Weymouth's history) plus a brewing exhibition. On the map, the triangle of land behind the brewery is today the traffic island opposite the end of Newton's Road – the road built in the 1890s as part of a planned Great Western Railway port in Newton's Cove which never materialised.

Most of the empty ground shown opposite Bloomfield Terrace (now part of Rodwell Avenue) and Spring Road was later built on, the most recent of these developments being in the 1990s when the houses of 'The Maltings' and 'Barley Way' and a large car park took over most of the parcel of land numbered '342' on the map, previously the site of brewery buildings and allotments.

The magnificent red brick brewery built by John Groves and Sons in 1904.

The brewery with its modern extension, but otherwise little changed.

The brewery's towering chimney.

The line that Newton's Road would later follow is shown running alongside the Malt House on the map – it was part of unfulfilled Great Western Railway plans to open a new port in Newton's Cove in the 1890s.

The modern houses which fill the empty land shown on the map.

Union Workhouse 44

Rodwell Terrace

Letter Box

Belfield Terrace

Alms Houses

147

145

Rodwell Villa

141

143

146

W E Y M 142 O U T H

138

139

Lansdowne

137

Rodwell House

B.M. 81.2

182

190

191

Rodwell

195

140

Longhill House

183

184

Old Reservoir

Clearmount Terrace

194

Clearmount Ho.

Longhill Villa

Longfield House

M.P.

189

Clearmount

186

187

188

192

C.B.

B.S.

MAP 26

ORDNANCE SURVEY 1864 (Scale 25″= 1 mile) WEYMOUTH : Rodwell

Buxton Road runs along the bottom of this section of the 1864 Ordnance Survey map, Wyke Road across the top. The new Weymouth and Portland Railway line passes under both roads, although the train service hadn't started at this date, the line opening in October 1865. Rodwell Station would open on this stretch of the line in 1870. The two roads, once known as the 'Upper' and 'Lower' Roads to Wyke, are linked by Rodwell Road, also known as Longhill Road, hence the house names incorporating Longhill and also Clearmount, the name for the general area at the base of the map.

The latter half of the nineteenth century saw the beginnings of the growth of Rodwell as a suburb of Weymouth. Rodwell Terrace, on the corner of St Leonard's Road (then still known as Union Road) no longer exists nor does Rodwell Villa: its replacement is illustrated below. Rodwell House, an early nineteenth century house built by local architect James Hamilton, is now the Rodwell House Hotel. The open ground opposite would later be filled with the houses of Rodwell Avenue. Longhill House is now divided into two dwellings, Nos. 58 (known as 'Beulah') and 56. Longfield House gave its name to Longfield Road, Longhill Villa later became the home of artist William Pye and next door was Clearmount House, then the vicarage for Holy Trinity church. Opposite, unnamed on the map, is Elwell Manor. Then its grounds were extensive; today the old house sits between New Close Gardens and Elwell Manor Gardens, two roads built on its former gardens. Right on the corner, a house was extensively damaged during a World War Two air raid and the ruins were removed and the road widened in 1963.

Rodwell Station, opened in 1870, was to be built on the railway line between Wyke Road and Buxton Road.

Sir Daniel Gooch of the Great Western Railway knew Weymouth well and visited the town both in his official capacity as Chairman of the GWR (when he was overseeing preparations on board the steamship *Great Eastern* prior to her transatlantic cable-laying voyages) and as a holiday visitor.

Holidaying here in 1881, his diary entry for Tuesday 27th December notes *'We walked to Wyke Regis this morning and back by way of Rodwell. This latter place is growing very fast. The views are beautiful, looking over Portland and the bay. Day fine.'*

The map shows four tiny almshouses opposite Lansdowne Square which were built in 1829 to accommodate four poor widows. They were demolished in 1957 and new bungalows in Rodwell Avenue replaced them. (*See MAP 33 for a larger plan of the Union Workhouse shown at the top of the map*)

Rodwell Villa also known as Rodwell Lodge, once the home of Sir John Groves, was a hotel before its demolition and replacement with the present 'Rodwell Lodge'

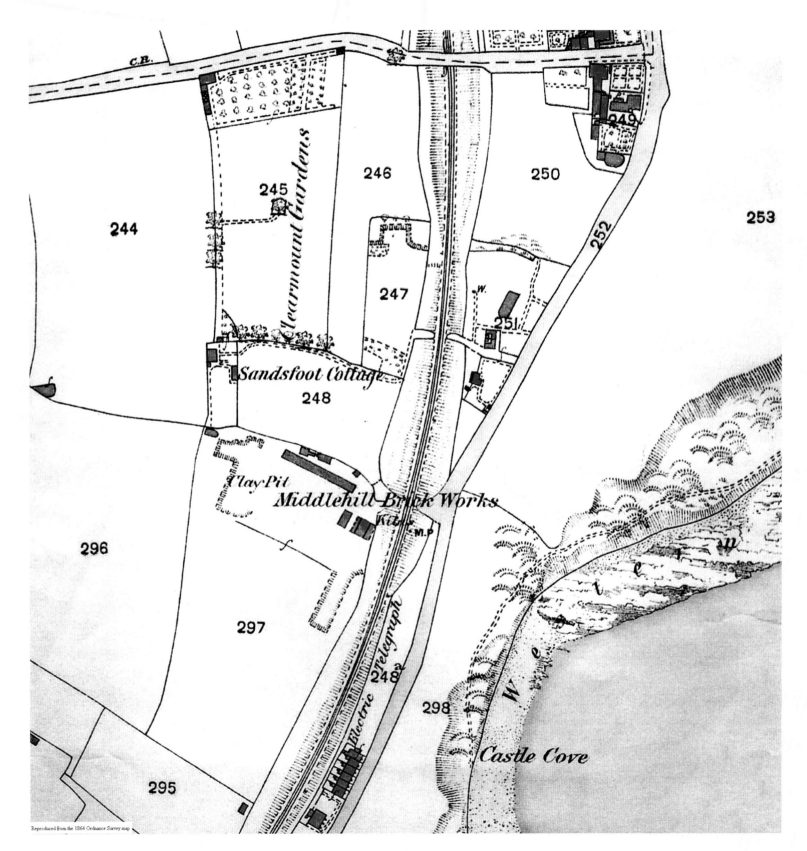

244

245

246

Clearmount Gardens

250

252

253

247

W.

251

Sandsfoot Cottage

248

296

Clay Pit

Middlehill Brick Works

Kiln M.P.

297

Electric Telegraph

248a

298

295

Castle Cove

MAP 27

ORDNANCE SURVEY 1864 (Scale 25″= 1 mile) WEYMOUTH : Rodwell

A final selection from the 1860s' 25″ = 1 mile Ordnance Survey maps is a continuation of the previous map. This time Buxton Road runs along the top of the map and its junction with Old Castle Road is shown top right. Running parallel with Old Castle Road is the line of the Weymouth and Portland Railway, opened in October 1865.

Standing on the Middlehill Brick Works site today, with its clay pit and kiln, you would see the houses of Sudan Road and the Old Castle public house of 1926. The earliest houses of Clearmount Road were built in the 1900s and followed the boundary line on the right hand side of Clearmount Gardens. Later developments in Clearmount Road were part of the Southlands Estate of the 1930s.

Marine Terrace, comprising the six houses at the bottom of the picture, is of early nineteenth century date (now Nos. 70-80 Old Castle Road). Behind this terrace can be found a trace of Sandsfoot Castle Halt, opened in 1932 on Weymouth and Portland Railway and now part of the Rodwell Trail footpath and cycle way which follows the line of the disused railway from Westham to Wyke Regis.

The Old Castle Hotel of 1926 stands on part of the former brickyard site.

A new sign on the Rodwell Trail at the site of Sandsfoot Halt, opened in 1932 (the Weymouth and Portland Railway line closed to passengers in 1952, goods in 1965).

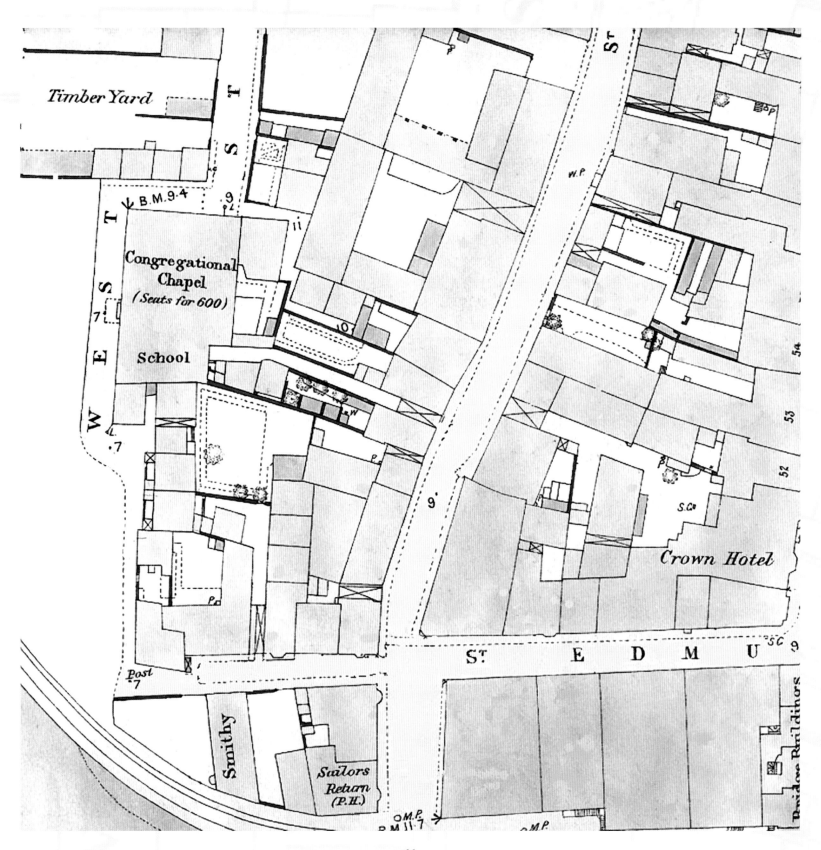

Timber Yard

WEST ST

B.M.9·4

Congregational
Chapel
(Seats for 600)

School

Crown Hotel

S.Cº

St EDMU

Smithy

Sailors
Return
(P.H.)

Post

B.M 11·7

W.P.

Bridge Buildings

MAP 28
ORDNANCE SURVEY 1864 (Scale 10.56 feet = 1 mile)
WEYMOUTH : Town centre (Ferry's Corner)

In 1855 the Ordnance Survey introduced a new large scale for the mapping of urban areas (usually towns with a population of more than 4000). This was the 1:500 scale or 10.56 feet = 1 mile. In 1863-4 Weymouth was surveyed at this scale and a set of 13 large coloured maps in landscape format was published, each map being just over 3 feet by 2 feet (96.6 cm x 64.4 cm). Some revision was carried out in the 1880s. Mapping in this very detailed large scale was discontinued after 1910. These superb maps were sold uncoloured (2 shillings each) or coloured (4 shillings each).

The Weymouth town maps are invaluable, providing a record of town streets and buildings in the mid-Victorian period. Full-size colour extracts from three of them follow, plus two reproduced at a slightly reduced scale in order to locate and include a more complete area than would otherwise be possible in this book's format. These maps are an invaluable tool for the local historian, providing a wealth of detail about the layout of individual buildings and the gardens or grounds surrounding them, long-lost street and terrace names and transport links.

The first extract is of the area at the lower end of the Melcombe side of the harbour showing the junction of St Nicholas Street and St Edmund Street. The harbour side 'Smithy' in 1864 was that of James Ferry and this is still known as 'Ferry's Corner' today. The Crown Hotel was to be completely rebuilt in 1868 and has been extended over the years, the present red brick additions being added in the late 1920s when the Town Bridge was replaced. The bow-fronted Bridge Buildings, just visible bottom right, were also removed in the '20s when the present Town Bridge was built.

The Congregational chapel as built in 1804.

West Street has seen many changes, the Congregational chapel building of 1804 having had a variety of uses including that of theatre, foundry and cold store before its demolition in 1968 and replacement initially with a car park and much later by apartment blocks. Curving around the base of the map are the lines of the 1865 Weymouth Harbour Tramway, the railway link between the railway station and the pier. Now disused, the lines are occasionally in the news when they take the blame for traffic mishaps.

The rebuilt Crown Hotel of 1868...

...much extended in the late 1920s.

The Ferry's Corner area, extended since the map's date, with a 'special' on the Weymouth Harbour Tramway line in August 1993. The line closed to regular traffic in 1988.

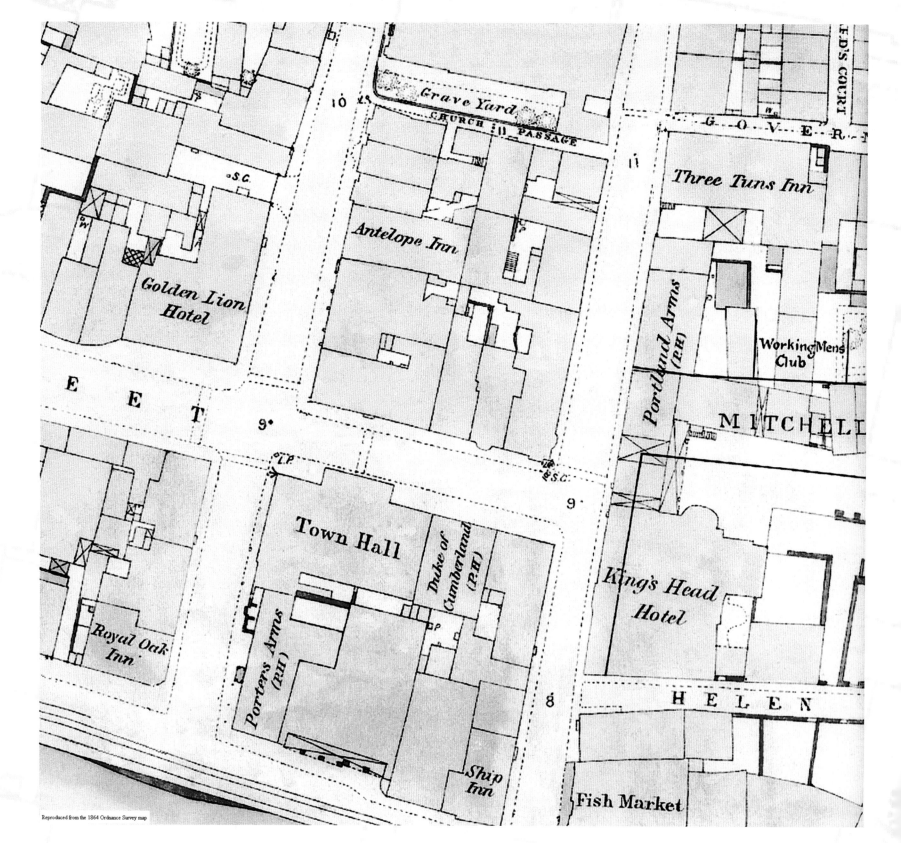

Reproduced from the 1864 Ordnance Survey map

68

MAP 29

ORDNANCE SURVEY 1864 (Scale 10.56 feet = 1 mile)
WEYMOUTH : Town centre (Guildhall)

Still on the Melcombe side, the 1864 map shows the continuation eastwards of St Edmund Street, with St Mary Street and Maiden Street running north/south.

A later owner of the map has drawn in the location of Mitchell Street – this new road linking East Street and Maiden Street was not completed until the 1870s.

Some of the pubs remain today, but the Porters Arms, the Antelope, the Portland Arms and the Three Tuns are long gone. The King's Head did not long survive the publication of the map as it was pulled down in the same decade to provide the site for Maiden Street Methodist church. The 'Town Hall' is more usually known as The Guildhall and a large brick warehouse which later incorporated the Porters Arms site stood behind it. Known as the Red Warehouse it was demolished in 1958 and an extension of the adjacent Ship Inn now fills the site.

In the map's top right hand corner the houses of Steward's Court were cleared in the late 1950s to provide the car park in East Street.

The 'Red Warehouse' once dominated the harbourside scene.

The Guildhall and Maiden Street Methodist church, which replaced the King's Head Inn shown on the map.

The disastrous fire of 17th January 2002, which gutted Maiden Street Methodist church.

The street scene in 2011 shows the ruined Methodist church, lost to fire in January 2002.

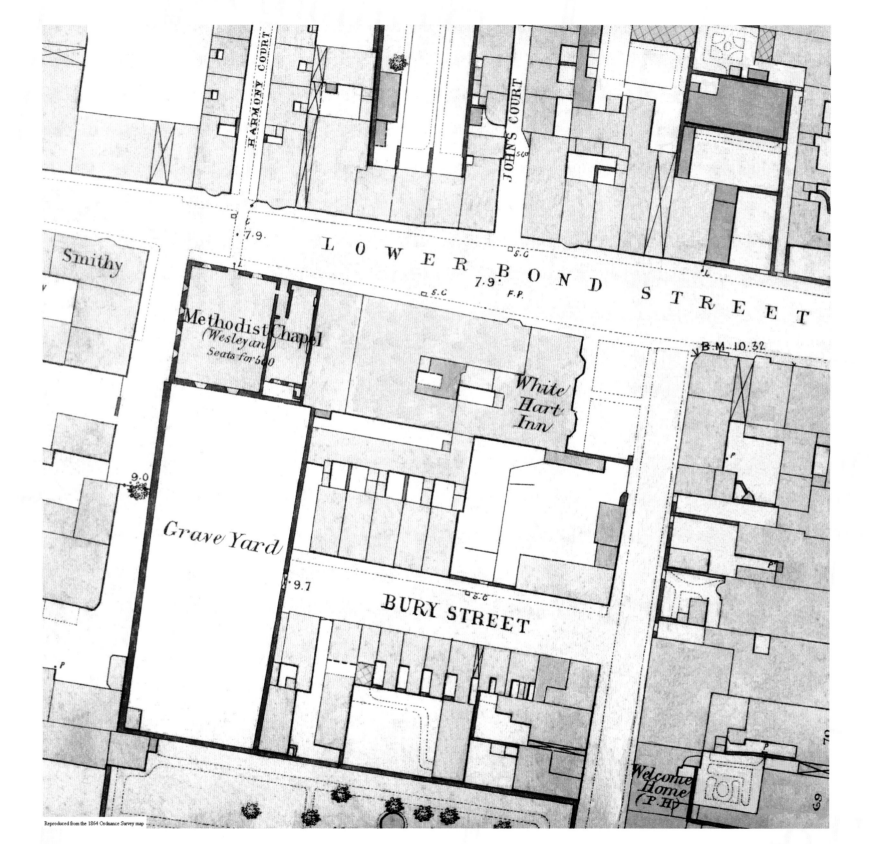

HARMONY COURT

JOHNS COURT

Smithy

7.9

L O W E R   B O N D   S T R E E T

7.9

F.P.

S.C.

S.C.

B.M. 10.32

Methodist Chapel
(Wesleyan)
Seats for 560

White
Hart
Inn

9.0

Grave Yard

9.7

S.C.

BURY STREET

Welcome
Home
(P.H)

G.9

MAP 30

ORDNANCE SURVEY 1864 (Scale 10.56 feet = 1 mile)
WEYMOUTH : Town Centre (Lower Bond Street and Bury Street)

A little further north, this section of the large scale 1864 map of the Melcombe side of the harbour takes us to an area much redeveloped in the latter years of the twentieth century. Much of Lower Bond Street was demolished and what remains is now incorporated into the New Bond Street shopping precinct. The seventeenth century White Hart Inn is probably the most recognisable feature here today. Neighbouring properties pulled down in the 1970s and 1980s included the Wesleyan Methodist chapel. It had long been redundant as a place of worship, having been replaced by Maiden Street Methodist church in the 1860s and in the twentieth century was in use as a store by local building firm Webb, Major.

Bury Street no longer exists. It once led to the little town graveyard shown on the map, but the area is now filled by a multi-screen cinema and car park. The remains of those who inhabited this little burial ground were re-interred in the cemetery at Westham.

On the north side of Lower Bond Street none of the buildings shown on the map stand now, all having been cleared in the 1980s prior to the long-delayed shopping redevelopment which finally opened in 2000. Many little courts leading off town streets have been lost over the years and here Harmony Court and John's Court were demolished.

The Welcome Home pub was in St Nicholas Street – the site now is the back entrance of a St Thomas Street shoeshop.

The present occupants of the site at the end of Bond Street. The White Hart Inn can be seen on the left.

These five cottages on the north side of Bury Street and the graveyard at the rear of the Methodist chapel are shown on the map. All the buildings on these two photographs have now gone.

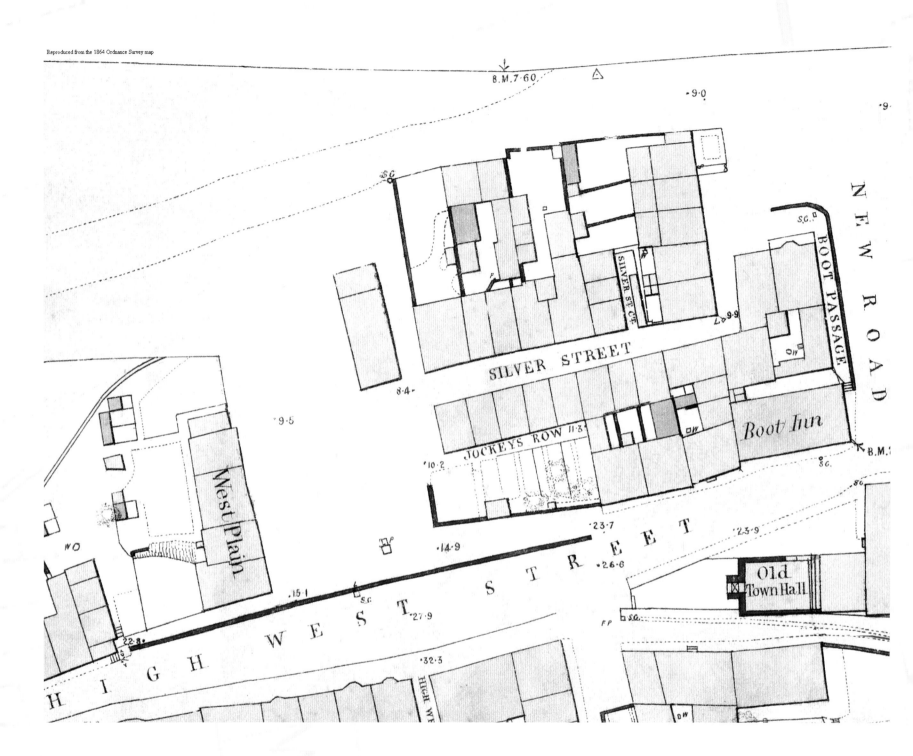

On the south side of the harbour in the 1860s were several little streets of terraced houses which were to be removed under a slum clearance order in the 1930s and replaced by the fire station on North Quay. Post WW2 years saw the clearance of many more buildings in this area, including the picturesque High Street where the council offices now stand.

Also lost to the town was a fine Tudor House on North Quay which was bulldozed in 1961 despite many objections and a Public Inquiry,

The site below the Old Town Hall, partially cleared in the 1930s.

which found against preserving it. Two ancient buildings shown on the map survive today – the Boot Inn and the Old Town Hall, once the centre of local government for Weymouth in the days before Weymouth and Melcombe Regis were forced into an initially unwelcome union in 1571.

West Plain was a row of cottages, also long gone and the whole of this corner at the bottom of Boot Hill was once known as 'The Plains of Weymouth'.

(*See* MAP 64 *for the buildings along North Quay and High Street before the 1961 demolitions*)

Two views of the Old Town Hall in the early eighteenth century, by John William Upham. The Victorians carried out considerable rebuilding and modernising in the 1890s.

The Fire Station of 1939 on North Quay, soon to be redundant when a new building opens on Radipole Lane.

WEST

Chapelry Tavern

B.M.66·37

Pillar Letter Box

FRANCHISE STREET

Salem Place

Bee Hive (P.H.)

Ebenezer Place

Prospect Place

Newtown Place

East Row

West Row

QUEEN'S PLACE

Concord Place

Cornopean Inn

Queen's Row

Southampton Row

Gordon Row

Wesleyan School Boys & Girls

B.M.58·66

58·3

58·2

Queey Pl

UNION ROAD

Union Place

B.M.58·09

WEYM

S P R I

74

MAP 32

ORDNANCE SURVEY 1864 (Scale 10.56 feet = 1 mile) WEYMOUTH : Chapelhay

Another extract from the 10.56 feet = 1 mile 1864 survey, slightly reduced in scale to enable the layout of the old streets of Chapelhay to be seen in some detail. Newcomers to the town today would recognise the names of Franchise Street and the Chapelhay Tavern, but little else. By the time the Second World War broke out in 1939, some properties here had been lost to slum clearance orders but the whole of the close-knit community of Chapelhay was devastated by wartime German bombs which destroyed or severely damaged many homes and caused the deaths of many residents. Lost for ever are terrace and street names such as

Newtown Place, Salem Place, Ebenezer Place, Concord Place and Queen's Row. The map shows 'Union Place' in Union Road, renamed St Leonard's Road in 1872, possibly because its residents preferred not to be linked to the 'Union', the workhouse on nearby Wyke Road (*see* next map).

In the 1950s, after many much-resented post-war delays, the Chapelhay ruins were completely cleared and local authority flats (Chapelhay Heights) and houses went up on the site. One of the streets was named Oakley Place and another Gordon Row as reminders of their blitzed predecessors.

Chapelhay from the air, the worst of the World War Two air raid damage clearly visible.

Oakley Place following the air raid of 9th May 1941 when seven people died and more than a hundred and fifty buildings were damaged, some beyond repair.

Chapelhay Heights, the flats which replaced the bombed buildings in the 1950s.

The Chapelhay Tavern, survivor of the World War Two bombs which fell here. It has also outlived its near neighbour of 1959, The Prospect public house which was demolished in 2011, its site being redeveloped as housing.

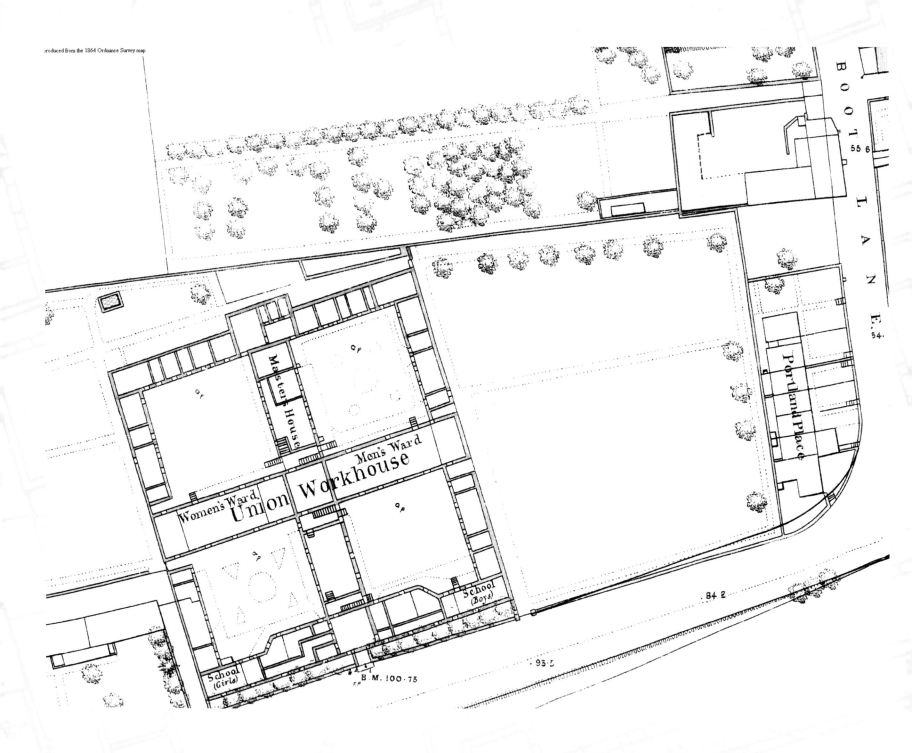

B O O T L A N E. 84.

55 6

Portland Place

Master House

Men's Ward

Women's Ward Union Workhouse

School (Boys)

School (Girls)

B.M. 100·73

84 2

93·5

MAP 33

ORDNANCE SURVEY 1864 (10.56 feet = 1 mile) WEYMOUTH : Workhouse

This section from the 1864 Ordnance Survey large-scale map is slightly reduced in scale to show the location of the Union Workhouse in Wyke Road, close to its junction with Boot Lane (today known as Boot Hill, although it is actually part of Rodwell Road).

Not every building's façade is lost once the original use of the building changes. Portwey Hospital and the apartments it has been converted into have hardly changed the appearance of the nineteenth century building. Little is known of day-to-day life in the workhouse as its records were pulped during the drive to salvage waste paper in World War Two.

The 'Union' was the amalgamation in the early 1830s of the various poor law institutions in the area which led to the building of this large 'Union Workhouse' to accommodate those unable to work and support themselves. It was no easy option and the conditions within were harsh to discourage people from seeking to enter it.

Workhouses were abolished in 1929 and the building was then administered by the County Council as 'Portwey', a hospital for unmarried mothers, the sick and the elderly. Casualties of the Second World War were treated here and post-war years saw the building converted to a maternity hospital – it was here in 'Portwey Hospital' that many local residents first saw the light of day. Following the closure of this facility in 1987, the building was converted to residential use in the early 1990s, with its imposing façade remaining unaltered. At the same time houses replaced twentieth century hospital buildings which had occupied the empty ground shown on the map around the workhouse.

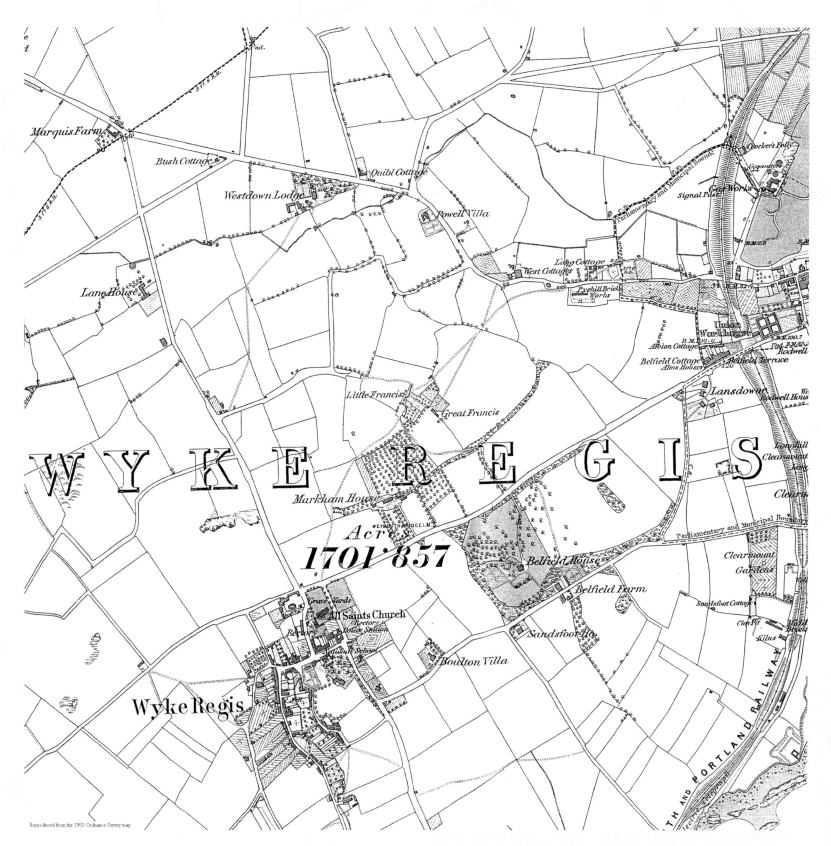

MAP 34

ORDNANCE SURVEY 1864 (Scale 6″ = 1 mile) WEYMOUTH : Pye Hill

A section from the 6″ = 1 mile Ordnance Survey map of 1864 (*see also* MAP 20) shows a large area west of the town which at that time was still within the parish of Wyke Regis. (The borough boundary can be followed on the right-hand side of the map – the dotted line of the 'Parliamentary and Municipal Boundary'.)

Marquis Farm (top left) stands at the junction of Chickerell Road and Lanehouse Rocks Road (the road takes its name from Lane House Farm and the rocks of the stone quarries depicted alongside the road closer to Wyke Regis, just below the large letter K of Wyke).

Along Chickerell Road Westdowne Lodge still stands, once the home of the Chimmo family. Captain William Chimmo's daughter Alice became Lady Peter when her husband was knighted and they moved into Westdowne in the early 1920s. Lady Peter died in 1950, having stayed on in the family home after her husband's death in 1939.

Quibo is spelt Quibl on the map. This place name is something of a mystery – did a former seafaring owner return from the Coiba Islands (formerly Quibo Islands) and name his property after them? Pyehill Brick Works provide another mystery place name – Pye is a local surname of the late-nineteenth and twentieth centuries – Will Pye was an artist, Bartle Pye an oil and seed merchant and twice Mayor of Weymouth, so perhaps there were earlier Pyes here.

Markham House in the centre of the map, was owned by the Swaffield family in the 1860s and overlooks the fields of the former Francis Farm, the green open space which is currently under threat of development.

See MAP 39 for a large scale coloured version of the Wyke village plan shown here.

The scene in 2011. The Railway Arch Hotel has been converted to apartments.

St Martin's C of E church built for the Holy Trinity congregation who lived in the Pye Hill area in 1908. Converted to apartments in the 1980s.

The railway bridge over Chickerell Road at Pye Hill – there are no trains now on the Weymouth and Portland Railway line, only walkers and cyclists on the Rodwell Trail from Westham to Wyke Regis.

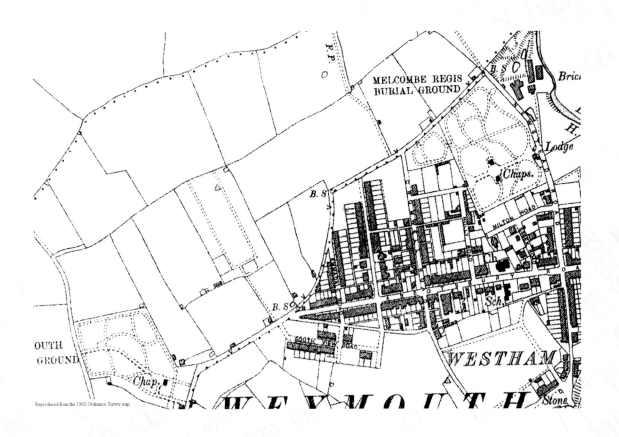

ORDNANCE SURVEY MAPS 1902 and 1929 : WESTHAM

More of Westham's green fields disappeared between the publication of these two Ordnance Survey maps of 1902 and 1929. The maps illustrate two very different styles of development. The size of the plots on the 1902 map indicate that the intention of the late-nineteenth century builders of Westham's earliest houses seems to have been to cram as many terraces as possible into streets which branch off Abbotsbury Road.

Contrast these plots with the sizeable ones on the lower map, provided when new local authority housing was built at Westham following the peace of 1918. Australian troops were in temporary camps where houses now stand and street names on the lower map are a reminder of their stay here – Melbourne Street, Sydney Street, Adelaide Crescent, Perth Street and Queensland Road. Sadly, some of the Aussie and New Zealand troops who were wounded at Gallipoli and hospitalised locally never returned home and they lie in the nearby Melcombe Burial Ground, shown on the map, where a fine memorial cross commemorates their sacrifice. The new estate is encompassed by Kitchener Road, named after Lord Kitchener, the famous general who is also remembered for the striking 'Your Country Needs You!' First World War recruitment posters. He, too, was a casualty of the war, lost at sea when the ship he was on struck a mine.

When spare ground in Melcombe ran out and there was no room for a much-needed cemetery, the new Melcombe Regis burial ground of 1856 opened at Westham, in what was then Wyke Regis parish. Some of the great and good of the town lie here, an interesting collection of monuments.

The monument to Sir Henry Edwards (1820-1897), whose statue stands on Weymouth seafront.

The Commonwealth War Graves Commission cross commemorates the Anzac troops of World War One who died whilst here. Many had been severely wounded at Gallipoli in 1915.

The headstone of one of the Australian soldiers. It bears the badge of the Australian Imperial Forces and he was J. B. Burns, 24 years old and a private in the First Australian Pioneers.

ORDNANCE SURVEY 1903 and 1926/27 (with 1938 revisions) : WESTHAM

Sometimes this telescopic gas storage facility towers over the harbourside, at other times, as here, if not exactly unobtrusive it is not of landmark height.

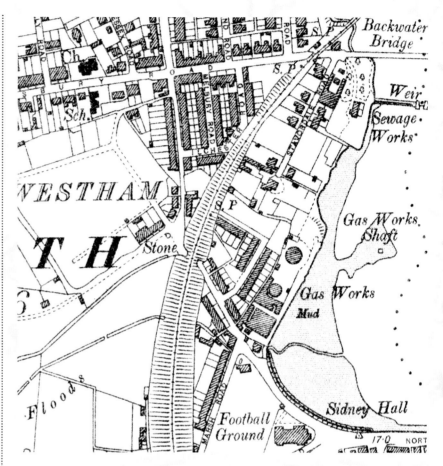

Moving closer to Westham Bridge and the Backwater these two maps illustrate the important industrial sites which once occupied the inner harbour shore. The earlier map of 1903 (above) pre-dates the construction of Westwey Road. A road to connect the Backwater Bridge and North Quay was under discussion for many years but it was 1930 before Westwey Road opened to traffic and as can be seen here, the gas works in 1903 overlooked a muddy shoreline. Pipes in a tunnel conveyed the gas to the Melcombe side of the town and the tunnel's shaft appears on many later maps of the Backwater – it was not removed until 1995.

The town in 1903 had no electricity supply, but the dense black area of buildings north of the gas works on the second map is the site of the Electricity Generating Station, which began operating in September 1904. Close to the bridge (the 1859 timber Backwater Bridge on the first map, the present Westham Bridge of 1921 on the second) are the sewage works and yard of the borough council – which also operated both gas and electricity works until nationalisation in 1948.

The later map shows Westwey Road and the large area of the Backwater reclaimed to provide the site for this new road and also additional land for an expanding gas works. None of the gasometers shown on the maps exist today – the rather unlovely one which stands close to Westwey Road today dates from 1957.

Close to the bridge, the Weir shown was part of a Victorian dam. At a time when the town refused to properly tackle the problems of sewage disposal, the dam was intended to flush out the inner harbour where the contents of house privies and cess pits which were daily tipped into it caused unpleasant sights and smells. Long redundant, the hefty stone dam was removed in 1995.

(*Compare these maps with* MAP 19, (1857) *and* MAP 65 (1956))

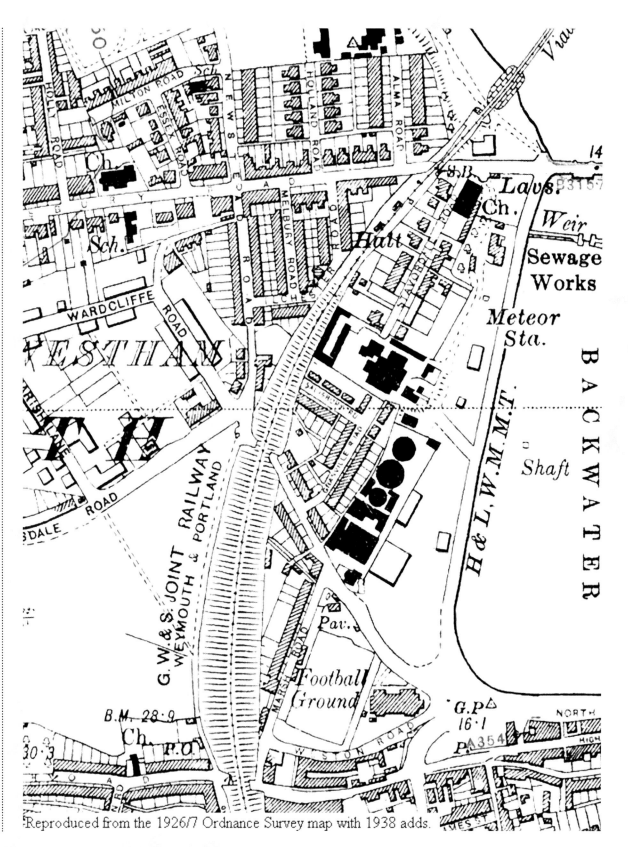

Reproduced from the 1926/7 Ordnance Survey map with 1938 adds.

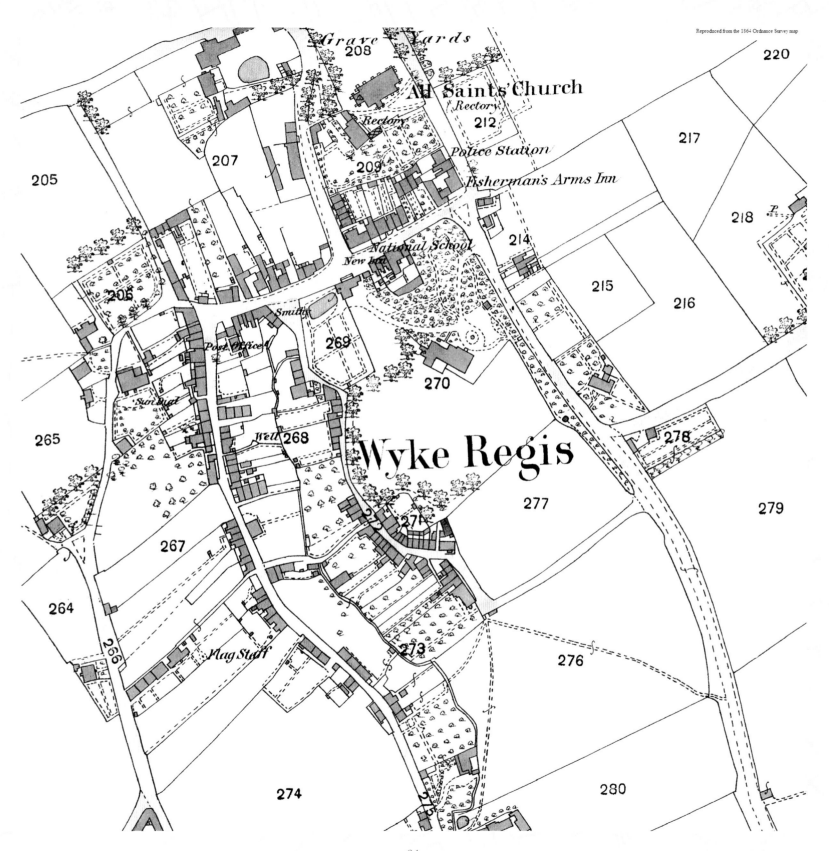

220

217

218   P.

205

207

208

All Saints' Church

Rectory

Rectory   212

Police Station

209

Fisherman's Arms Inn

214

205

National School

New Inn

215   216

Smithy

269

265

Sun Dial

Post Office

Well   268

270

Wyke Regis

277

278

279

267

264

266

Flag Staff

273

271

274   275

276

280

MAP 39

ORDNANCE SURVEY 1864 (Scale 25″= 1 mile) WYKE REGIS : Wyke Village

A very undeveloped Portland Road runs north-south on the right-hand side of this Wyke village map, another section from the 25″= 1 mile Ordnance Survey of 1864. This is 'old Wyke', the ancient settlement south of the River Wey, which pre-dates its now larger neighbour Weymouth. The Fisherman's Arms building on the corner of Portland Road and Chamberlaine Road still stands, although no longer a pub. Close by, the former Police Station has also now been converted to a dwelling, known as Church Cottage.

On the left, the former Fisherman's Arms pub and on the right, the cottage which was once the Police Station.

in ancient churches. The Rectory shown still stands, although incumbents in the twentieth century moved to a new building in Portland Road.

Chamberlaine Road links Portland Road and High Street, with the 'Smithy' indicating Wyke Square, leading into the narrow and sharply angled Shrubbery Lane. Wyke House (beside the field number 270 on the map) was an early-nineteenth century building converted to a hotel in the 1920s and demolished in 1974: the houses of Wooland Gardens stand on its site.

On the far left of the map High Street runs into Westhill Road, where, at the very base of the map the triangular shape coloured pink indicates the curious design of Wyke Castle, not a castle at all, but a private dwelling designed for a local doctor in the 1850s.

Wyke's population would greatly increase at the beginning of the twentieth century after the establishment at Ferrybridge of Robert Whitehead's Torpedo Works. (see MAPS 40, 41, and 42)

Wyke church has changed little in these views of the early nineteenth and late twentieth centuries.

The fifteenth century parish church of All Saints is on the site of an earlier church. It dates to 1455 and is as originally built, having escaped the designs of the Victorian 'improvers' who destroyed many original features

Wyke House Hotel – the building can be seen in the background of the earlier Wyke church picture.

WYKE REGIS

Reproduced from the 1959 Ordnance Survey map

86

MAP 40

ORDNANCE SURVEY 1959 WYKE REGIS : Portland Road

This late 1950s map was published almost a century after the map of Wyke village (MAP 39). The road junction just seen at the centre top of the map is Foord's Corner (it is also on MAP 39 of Wyke village in 1864, the plot labelled 278 on the right hand side. One of the buildings shown was probably the cottage belonging to the Foord family who gave their name to this area).

The original Victorian school building at the far end of Victoria Road.

Foord's Corner – the scene in the 1880s before Portland Road was built up ... and in 2011.

The development of houses off Portland Road, in formerly empty fields between Ferrybridge and 'old Wyke', began in 1891 when Whitehead's Torpedo Factory opened, the first industry in this rural area and the beginning of the ribbon development along and on both sides of Portland Road. Early buildings on its west side in Gallwey Road, Parkmead Road and Victoria Road probably housed Whitehead's workers (Gallwey Road takes its name from the works' first manager, Captain Edwin Payne

Gallwey; Park Mead from the farm here).

The school at the end of Victoria Road (since replaced) was built by the Whitehead Company. By 1900 houses were appearing in Williams Avenue and Sunnyside Road (the original plan had been to name this Fair View Road and today it is the short street linking the two which is known as Fairview). The Weymouth and Portland Railway line was a long way from old Wyke and when Wyke Regis Halt opened in 1909 it was intended to serve the factory rather than the village, although residents there did benefit from an early railway-operated bus service.

Almost all the open land on the eastern side of Portland Road disappeared in the 1950s when the Downclose housing estate was laid out (its streets easily recognisable as all bear place names beginning with the letter 'D').

Wyke Regis Halt on the Weymouth and Portland Railway, opened in 1909 close to the Whitehead works at Ferrybridge.

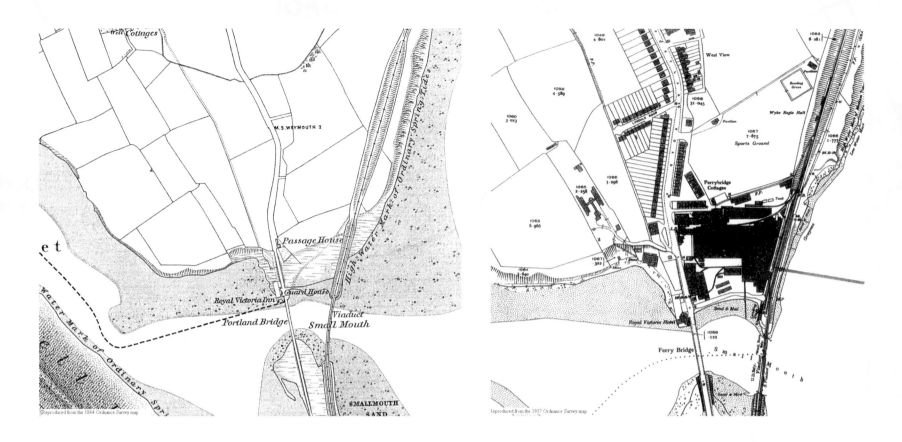

Reproduced from the 1864 Ordnance Survey map

Reproduced from the 1937 Ordnance Survey map

The original buildings of Robert Whitehead's Torpedo
Works at Ferrybridge, opened in 1891.

ORDNANCE SURVEY 1863 and 1937 WYKE REGIS : Ferrybridge

Maps more than seventy years apart show very different views of the Ferrybridge area of Wyke Regis.

On the first map 'Portland Bridge' was the first road bridge to cross Smallmouth. Made of timber, it opened in 1839 and the original Royal Victoria Inn dates from the same time. From the 'Guard House', troops patrolled the bridge to prevent any escape attempts by the convict workforce engaged in quarrying stone for the construction of Portland Breakwaters, work on which commenced in 1849. Also shown is the 'Passage House' where folk wanting to reach the island in earlier years had waited for the ferryboat to take them across the water (pictures of the Smallmouth Ferry can be found accompanying MAP 5). The second bridge, also of timber, was new when the map was drawn and carried the line of the Weymouth and Portland Railway, opened in 1865.

By 1937 the second map shows that the former rural scene at Ferrybridge had completely changed. In 1891 industry arrived in Wyke Regis with the opening of Robert Whitehead's torpedo factory, the workshops filling the large site shown, with its adjacent Sports Ground and a pier in Portland Harbour. Wyke Regis Halt, some way from the original old Wyke village, opened in 1909 to serve the factory. Houses began to stretch back along Portland Road once the works opened.

The two bridges shown on the later map were steel replacements of the original timber structures, but both have also now gone – the road bridge of the 1890s was replaced by a new bridge opened in 1984 and located slightly closer to Portland, and the rail bridge of 1902, redundant following the closure of the line in 1965, was removed in 1971.

Houses of the Harbour Point development now fill the former Ferrybridge industrial site.

Three pictures are all of the second Ferrybridge which carried road traffic to Portland – it was replaced by a third Ferrybridge in a position closer to Portland in 1984. The first aerial view looks towards Wyke and clearly shows the gap left at Smallmouth when the rail bridge was removed in 1971. The second, from the opposite direction, shows the extensive Whitehead's site. Vickers Armstrong, Wellworthys and AE Pistons followed, but industry left in 1993 and the buildings were demolished.

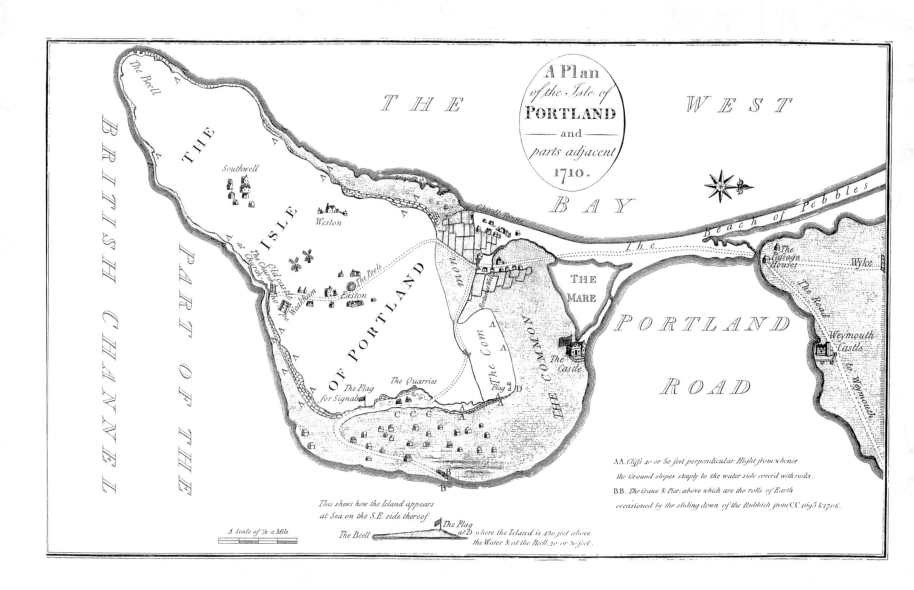

A Plan of the Isle of **PORTLAND** and parts adjacent 1710.

THE WEST BAY

BRITISH CHANNEL

THE PART OF THE

THE ISLE

OF PORTLAND

The Beell

Southwell

Weston

Old Castle
at The Church
The Church

The Weadsum

The Poole

Easton

The Flag
for Signals

The Quarries

Chisill Banke

Fortification

The Com
The Flag

THE COMMON

THE MARE

The Castle

PORTLAND

ROAD

Beach of Pebbles
The
to Weymouth
The Road

The Passage
Houses

Wyke

Weymouth Castle

AA. Cliffs 40 or 50 feet perpendicular Hight from whence
the Ground slopes steeply to the water side coverd with rocks.
BB. The Crane & Pier, above which are the rolls of Earth
occasioned by the sliding down of the Rubbish, from CC 1695 & 1708.

This shews how the Island appears
at Sea on the S.E. side thereof

A Scale of ½ a Mile

The Beell

The Flag
at D where the Island is 430 feet above
the Water & at the Beell, 20 or 30 feet.

MAP 43

PORTLAND MAP, 1710

From John Hutchins' *The History and Antiquities of the County of Dorset*

Having reached Ferrybridge, the next location is Portland and this map, which appeared in the 1774 first edition and the two subsequent editions of John Hutchins' *History of Dorset* shows the island in 1710, more than a century before the first bridge was built to connect it to the mainland at Wyke Regis. Portland, although always known as 'The Island and Royal Manor of Portland' is geographically a peninsula since Chesil Beach connects it to the mainland at Abbotsbury some ten miles along the coast, but to all intents and purposes for those living locally it was an 'island' and had to be reached by crossing the water at the point known as 'Smallmouth'. The Passage Houses shown on the map offered shelter at this exposed spot for those awaiting the ferryboat. *(Illustrations of the ferry can be found accompanying MAP 5)*

The two Tudor Castles standing guard over Portland Roads were part of King Henry VIII's south coast chain of defences against attack from Europe in the sixteenth century. From the mid-nineteenth century ships seeking shelter here would have the protection of the massive breakwaters which enclose Portland Harbour today, with their associated forts and defence works. Some of 'The Common' would later be given up to provide the site for the Verne Citadel, part of these Victorian government works. Today's place names are all recognisable – Portland Bill or 'The Beell' is derived from the shape of the southern tip of the island which resembles a bird's beak or bill – rather appropriate as one of the disused lighthouses here is today one of the UK's best-known bird observatories.

(Above and right) The two Tudor guardians of Portland Roads before the nineteenth century breakwaters and forts provided shelter and defences here. Portland Castle is in fine condition today, but Sandsfoot Castle's cliff edge site has been undermined by the sea over the centuries. Both views are from around 1800.

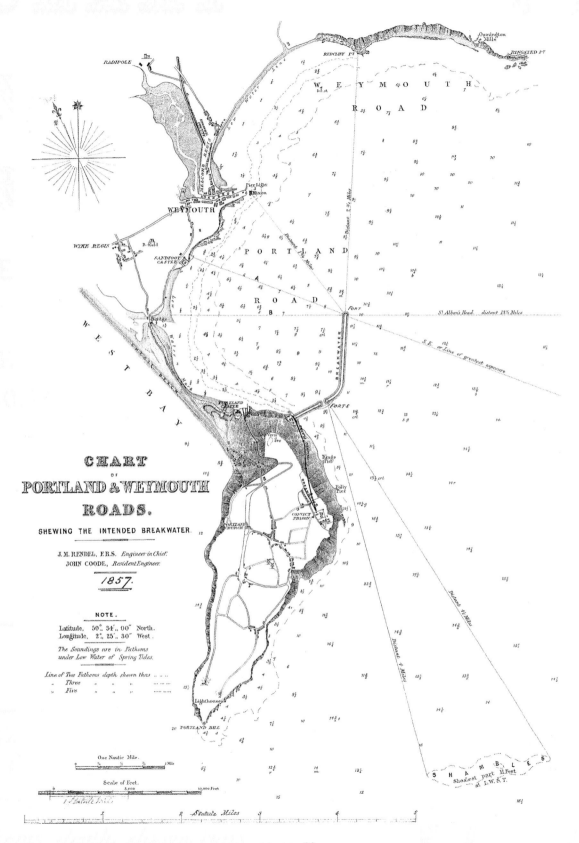

CHART
OF
PORTLAND & WEYMOUTH
ROADS.

SHEWING THE INTENDED BREAKWATER.

J. M. RENDEL, F.R.S. *Engineer in Chief.*
JOHN COODE, *Resident Engineer.*

1857.

NOTE.

Latitude, 50°. 34′. 00″ North.
Longitude, 2°. 25′. 30″ West.

*The Soundings are in Fathoms
under Low Water of Spring Tides.*

Line of Two Fathoms depth shewn thus ....
„   Three   „   „   „   „ ....
„   Five   „   „   „   „ ....

One Nautic Mile.

Scale of Feet.

MAP 44

CHART OF PORTLAND AND WEYMOUTH ROADS SHEWING THE INTENDED BREAKWATER, 1857

This chart shows the line of Portland Breakwater, construction of which began in 1849 – a massive project which was not completed until 1872. The plan appears to have the date of 1857 added by hand, although it is probably correct as the convict prison and inclined plane from the stone quarries to the breakwater works appear to be well established and the top left-hand corner shows the main line railway, which opened to Weymouth in that year.

The initial breakwater project consisted of two arms extending out from Portland and was part of a series of fortifications to protect the south coast which came to be known as 'Palmerston's Follies' after the Victorian Prime Minister who supported the scheme although the expected attack from France never came. The local defences included the breakwaters, the Nothe Fort at Weymouth and the Verne Citadel at Portland as well as coastal gun emplacements and a fort at Upton, near Osmington. The breakwaters themselves were also completed with substantial forts.

This vast, inevitably noisy and disruptive construction project was initially a cause of some concern in Weymouth as it was felt that prospective holidaymakers might be discouraged from visiting what was then a genteel resort still basking in its glory days as King George III's favourite holiday town. In fact the opposite was true, and contemporary illustrations show that these enormous building works became something of a tourist attraction themselves, with unconcerned visitors strolling about construction sites which today would be fenced-off, 'hard hats must be worn' and 'unauthorised entry prohibited' areas. The foundation stone of the breakwaters was laid by Prince Albert on 25th July 1849 (it was actually dropped into the sea with a thunderous splash which soaked the first few rows of distinguished guests invited to witness the ceremony). The Prince Consort maintained his interest in the project and visited Portland several times before his death in 1861. When the project was declared complete in 1872, it was his son Albert Edward, Prince of Wales (later King Edward VII) who came to Portland and the magnificent memorial he unveiled to commemorate the event is illustrated below.

As time went on and submarine and torpedo development advanced, it was realised that the enclosure of the whole of Portland Roads was vital for the protection of shipping and in the 1890s the building of two more breakwaters was commenced extending out from Bincleaves on the Weymouth side, a project which took some ten years to complete.

John Harvey's proposed breakwater was illustrated in his pamphlet *'Remarks on the subject of a breakwater for Portland Roads'* re-published by his son in 1827 long before the government works commenced.

The Prince of Wales laid the final stone of the Portland Breakwater project on 10th August 1872.

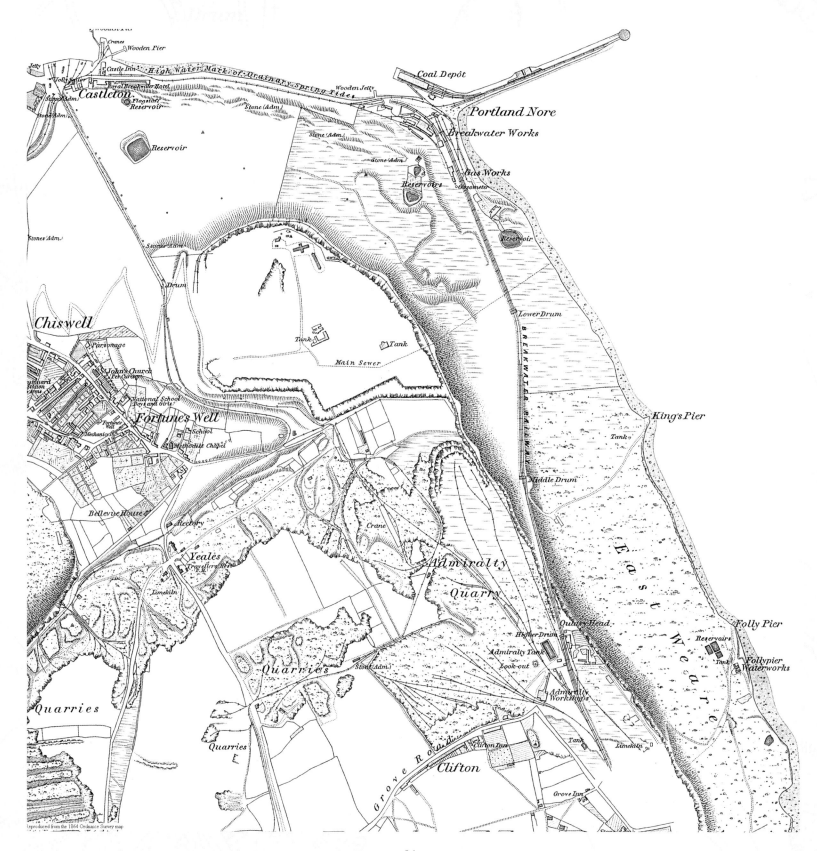

MAP 45

ORDNANCE SURVEY 1864 : PORTLAND

To assist with the mammoth task of building the Portland Breakwaters, convicts were brought to the island in 1848. They were first engaged in the construction of prison buildings and then in the quarrying and dressing of stone as well as working on the actual breakwater and fortifications. These men had been sentenced to transportation, but had their sentences divided into three parts, the first involving a spell in a closed prison, the second a prison term which included time spent on 'public works', which, if completed in exemplary fashion would entitle them to earn wages and other privileges of freedom when they were transported to the Colonies to serve the third part of their sentences.

The map shows the Admiralty Quarry, some 400 feet

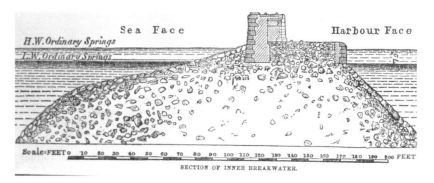

Sea Face — Harbour Face

H.W. Ordinary Springs
L.W. Ordinary Springs

Scale:FEET 0 10 20 30 40 50 60 70 80 90 100 110 120 130 140 150 160 170 180 190 200 FEET
SECTION OF INNER BREAKWATER.

Building up the breakwater profile.

Convicts at work in the Portland quarries.

above sea level, and the Breakwater Railway which conveyed the stone down to the breakwater works. This incline railway consisted of three slopes, each about 1,500 feet long. Each slope had a double set of rails and was worked by a wire rope passing over a drum connecting two trains of wagons, the full train drawing up the empty train of wagons as it descended. At the foot of the incline the wagons were conveyed out to sea via a massive timber staging wide enough to support five or six lines of rails. Holes between the rails enabled each wagon to be positioned so that when its trapdoor-like base was opened the 10-ton load of stone tumbled into the sea. In this way 2000-3000 tons of stone were deposited each day and as each section of the breakwater was filled and showed itself above the water, so the staging and rails progressed out to sea and the breakwater work advanced.

Railway lines atop a timber staging to carry the stone out to sea.

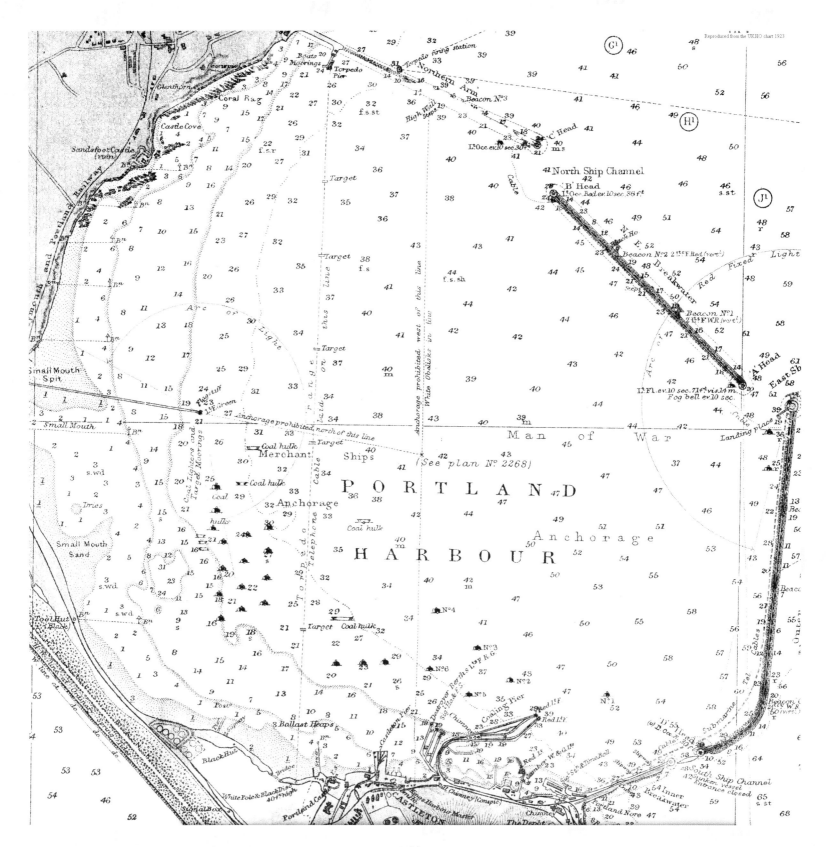

MAP 46

CHART OF WEYMOUTH AND PORTLAND
Published by the Admiralty Hydrographic Office, 1923

This complex Admiralty chart of the 1920s illustrates the completion of the enclosure of Portland Harbour: the original 'Portland Breakwater' built between 1849 and 1872 and actually consisting of two separate sections, stretches out from Portland. Construction of the two later breakwaters across the remaining open stretch of water from Bincleaves began in 1896 and was completed, apart from some finishing work, early in 1905. The newer breakwaters were completed in just over a third of the time it took to build the original two arms and the method of construction was quite different : there was no overhead railway, all the stone being conveyed from Portland to the site in specially constructed barges.

The outbreak of World War One in 1914 and the continuing development of submarine warfare had brought the realisation that the 'South Ship Channel' between the two Victorian breakwater arms close to Portland was vulnerable attack by enemy torpedoes and was thus a threat to any assembled Royal Navy vessels. As can be seen on the chart, the harbour entrances between the later breakwaters had been staggered to deter such attacks. It was decided close the South Ship Channel by sinking HMS *Hood*, an obsolete turret battleship built in 1891, to act as a blockship. *Hood* was positioned and sunk on 4th November 1914. The old ship turned over as she went down and now rests on the bottom with her keel uppermost, having effectively scuppered any plans there may have been to raise her when the war ended. Hence the 'Sunken vessel. Entrance closed' note on the chart.

A large number of coal hulks can be seen in the harbour but newer warships were oil-burning and two oil tanks had been built on The Common in the early 1900s (just visible as dark circles at the bottom of the chart) and later ones are shown on The Mere – there would eventually be twenty six in all. None remain. The Royal Navy left Portland in 1995 and the oil tanks were dismantled in 2008.

The old battleship HMS *Hood* positioned in the South Ship Channel ready for sinking in 1914...

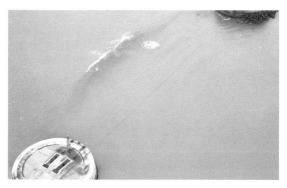

...where she still lies today.

In March 1901 during construction of the Bincleaves breakwaters the *Dinnington's* captain stranded his vessel on the new works at night and found his ship high and dry when the tide went down in the morning. The *Dinnington* was later successfully refloated.

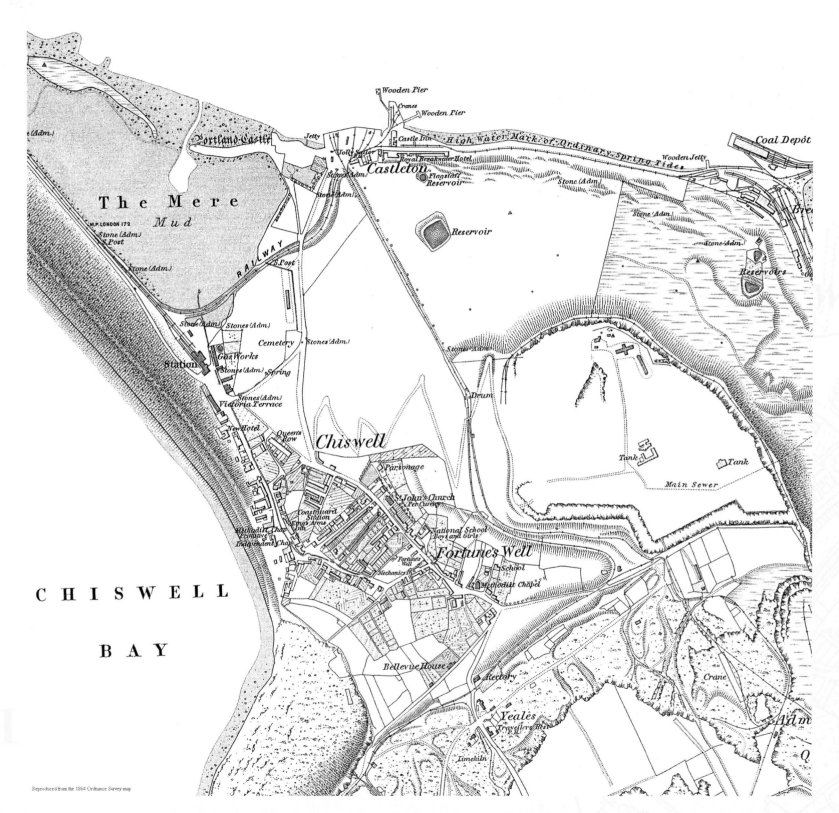

Reproduced from the 1864 Ordnance Survey map

MAP 47
ORDNANCE SURVEY 1864 : PORTLAND

Moving to the west side of Portland, two more island railways can be found on the 1864 map. In the centre is the Merchants' Incline, part of the Merchants' Railway, which carried stone from the privately-owned quarries at the top of the island down to Castletown Pier for onward shipment by sea. 'The Portland Railway Company' was authorised by Act of Parliament in 1825 and the Merchants' Railway opened in October 1826, the first railway of any type to be built in this part if the country. Always horse-drawn, it lasted until 1939. The incline operated on a similar 'drum' principle as described in the text which accompanies MAP45. Although the lines and associated buildings are long-gone, the steep slope of the Merchants' incline can still be seen on Portland today.

On the left-hand side of the map are Portland Station and the lines of the Weymouth and Portland Railway, built between 1862 and 1864, although its opening was delayed until October 1865. Stone was transferred from the horse-drawn Merchants' Railway to the new line via Castletown sidings. After many delays the railway was eventually extended as far as Easton in 1902. This section was wonderfully scenic, like much of the route from Weymouth. The line closed to passengers in 1952 and closed altogether in 1965 and few traces remain on the island now. Its history is fascinating and covered in depth in the four volumes of *Isle of Portland Railways* by B. L. Jackson (The Oakwood Press, 1999-2002).

An early 1900s picture postcard view from the bottom of the Merchants' Railway incline.

A loaded wagon ready to descend the Merchants' Railway incline. Horses had previously and with great difficulty hauled stone-laden carts down Portland's steep slopes.

Portland Station on the Weymouth and Portland Railway. Demolished in 1969.

MAP 48

ORDNANCE SURVEY 1864 : PORTLAND

A final extract from the 1864 Portland map takes the road up to Easton and Wakeham en route for Portland Bill, and shows Church Hope Cove ('Hope' and 'Ope' are both used on maps) with its trio of historic buildings : the ruins of St Andrew's, the oldest church on the island (the present St Andrew's – also known as 'Avalanche Church' after the 1877 shipwreck it commemorates – is at Southwell), the ancient fortification

Rufus Castle, sometimes known as Bow and Arrow Castle, and Pennsylvania Castle, not a castle at all, but a grand house built for John Penn in 1800.

There was a strong Methodist congregation on Portland in the nineteenth century and the maps locate a number of the chapels on the island.

Rufus Castle, a watercolour by local artist John William Upham whose paintings provide much detail about the local scene in the early nineteenth century.

John Penn's fine house, designed by James Wyatt, was completed in 1800. Fine views, but a dramatically steep flight of steps down to the cove below.

Making the descent to Church Ope Cove around 1900.

Reproduced from the 1864 Ordnance Survey map

102

Chickerell was once was easily identified from miles around by the tall chimneys of its two brickworks – Crook Hill, just off today's B3157 coast road to Bridport and Putton Brickworks off Putton Lane. The industry was well established by the mid-19th century and Chickerell bricks are recognisable by their harsh red colour and very hard consistency.

The second map dates from 1929 and shows considerably extended works at both locations, together with the workers' cottages of Brickyard Terrace adjacent to Crook Hill. Crook Hill was owned successively by the Crickmays, well-known Weymouth architects, John Bagg the builder who was thrice Mayor of Weymouth, local building firm Webb, Major and finally Mitchell & Sons of Salisbury. Putton Lane Brickworks in the 1860s belonged to J. Northover, then Brown Brothers of Weymouth and, after the failure of a syndicate which took them over in 1920, the brickworks were owned by Charles Dean and then the Mitchells of Bournemouth, trading as The Weymouth Brick and Tile Company.

Both brickworks closed in the 1960s. Their chimneys survived for some years but all had been demolished by the end of the twentieth century. Today Crook Hill is the site of a construction company and council depot and former brickfields have been transformed into the tranquil lakes of Bennetts Water Gardens. Practically all the empty land shown on the maps south of the original village between the main road and Putton Lane as far

down as Crook Hill has since been covered with houses and just to the south a new road – Hampshire Road – now slices across Putton Lane directly linking a vastly expanded Chickerell to Weymouth Way and the town centre.

East Chickerell (top right of the 1864 map) was the house and farm owned by the Jesty family and known as East Chickerell Court. The buildings were demolished in the 1960s and an electricity transformer station stands here now.

Montevideo House was built around 1800 and, today a nursing home, has been renamed The Queen Charlotte.

The once landmark chimneys of Chickerell's brickworks.

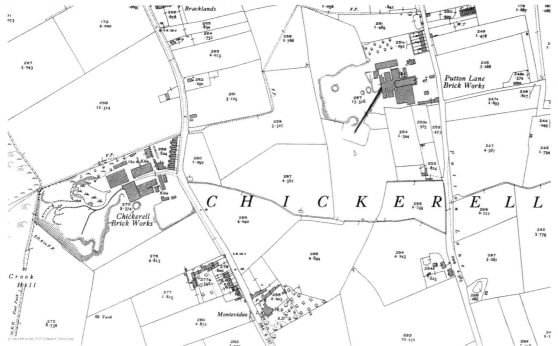

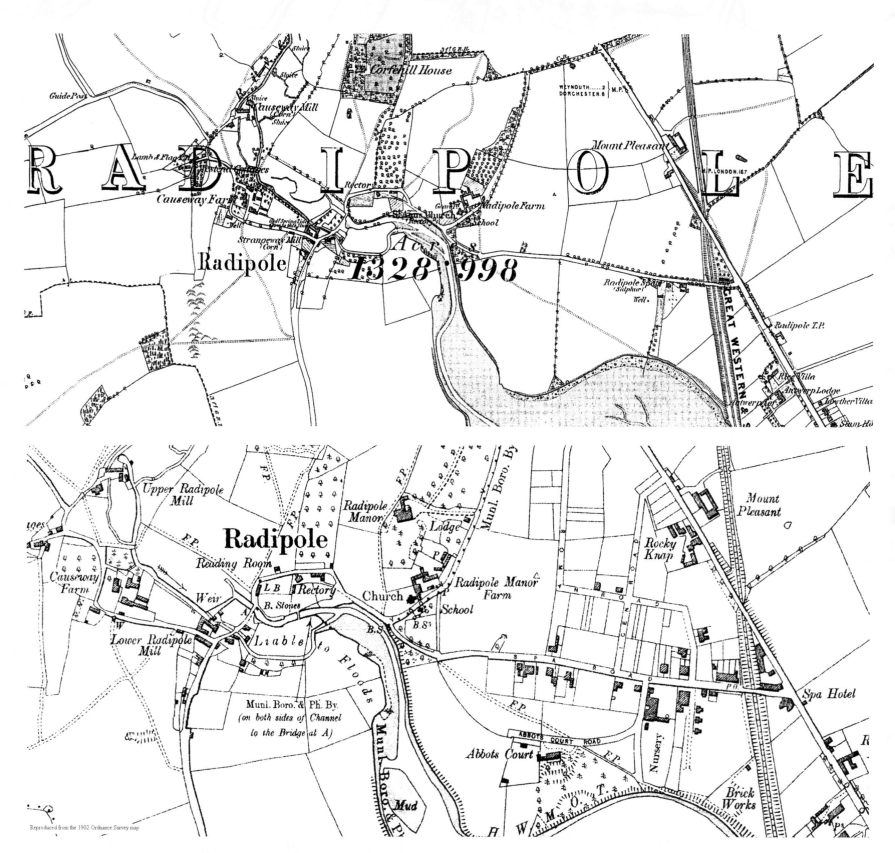

Reproduced from the 1902 Ordnance Survey map

ORDNANCE SURVEY 1864, 1902 and 1927 (with 1938 additions): RADIPOLE

Three Ordnance Survey maps spanning almost three quarters of a century illustrate the growth of what might be termed 'new' Radipole, off Dorchester Road and to the east of the old village.

The first map dates to 1864 and shows the then-unnamed Spa Road linking the main road and the original village. Sited along it in this rural setting is Radipole Spa, the establishment which gave the road its name. Although the spa was founded in the 1830s, the sulphurous waters were probably known about long before this date.

The spa was sold in 1898 and the second map, of 1902, shows developments and planned developments around its site. North of Spa Road, the intended road layouts of Roman Road and Icen Road can be seen. To the south Abbots Court Road (now Ullswater Crescent) led to the fine mansion belonging to local builder and three-times Mayor of Weymouth John Bagg, whose extravagant hospitality and lifestyle led to his bankruptcy in 1910. The house was demolished in 1987.

The third map, surveyed in 1927 with some amendments in 1938, shows a much more urban scene off Dorchester Road. Ullswater Crescent has been extended and lined with houses and terraces fill Queens Road and Kings Road (the site of the original spa was at the corner of Spa Road and Queens Road). The northern section of Roman Road has become Mount Pleasant Avenue, named after the old farm shown. Beyond this built-up area, the old Radipole village remains little changed.

Radipole Spa in its nineteenth century heyday…

…and the site today. These flats replaced a laundry on the spa site.

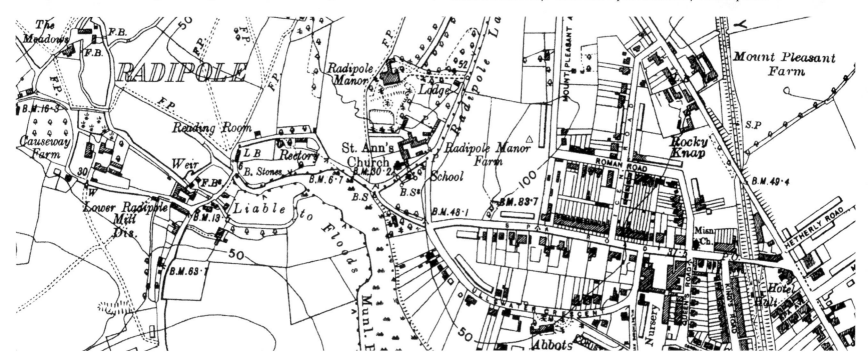

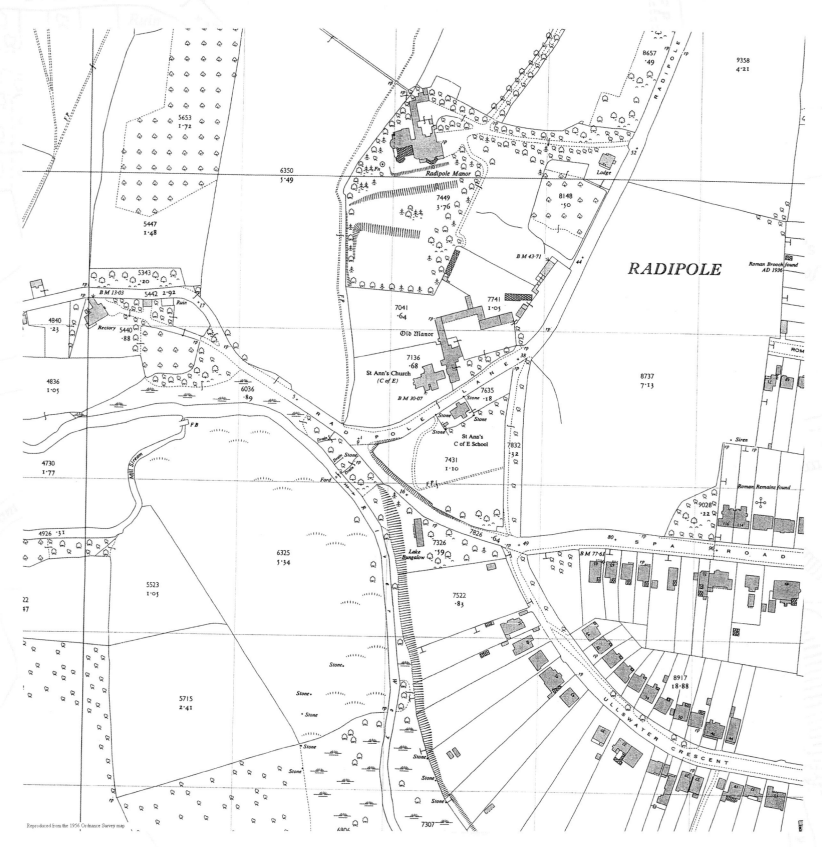

RADIPOLE

Reproduced from the 1956 Ordnance Survey map

106

MAP 54

ORDNANCE SURVEY 1956 : RADIPOLE

It is generally thought that the Romans sailed their craft up the River Wey to Radipole, where goods could be unloaded for onward transport to Dorchester (the Roman Durnovaria) by road. The exact route they took over the Ridgeway has not yet been discovered, but this 1950s' map indicates where some Roman artefacts were discovered when the Spa Road area was being developed in the early 1900s. These houses on the right-hand side of the map are part of the development of 'new' Radipole, spreading westwards to link up with the older village at the head of Radipole Lake.

When visiting the peaceful churchyard of St Ann's church with its birdsong and scampering squirrels, it is difficult to believe that it is alongside a busy stretch of Radipole Lane. The adjacent 'Old Manor' dates back at least to the sixteenth century. Beyond it stands the Victorian Radipole Manor, also known as West Mead and once the home of Richard ffolliot Eliot, one of two brothers who were partners in Eliot, Pearce and Co's Bank which crashed in 1897 with catastrophic consequences for many businesses and individuals in Weymouth. It was the sale of the brothers' extensive estate at Radipole prior to their bankruptcy which led to much of the development off the Dorchester Road in the early twentieth century.

Opposite the church and still in use when the map was published is the little school building of 1854 which closed in 1964, new buildings in Radipole Lane having replaced it.

The little former school building of 1854.

A rural scene looking towards Radipole St Ann's church in 1790 : one of John Love's series of local views.

Radipole church, little changed over the centuries.

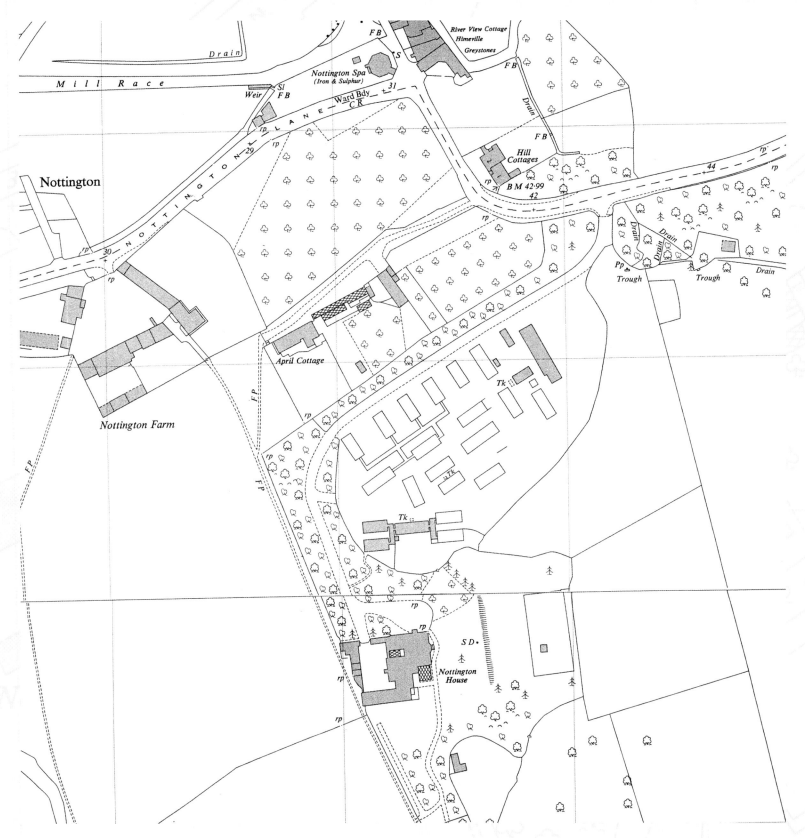

Nottington

Nottington Farm

April Cottage

Nottington House

Hill Cottages

River View Cottage
Himeville
Greystones

Nottington Spa
(Iron & Sulphur)

Mill Race

Drain

Weir

Sl
F B

F B

S

F B

F B

Ward Bdy
C R

B M 42·99

Trough

Trough

Pp

Drain

Drain

Drain

Drain

Tk

Tk

Tk

S D

FP

FP

FP

MAP 55
ORDNANCE SURVEY 1956 : NOTTINGTON

Nottington's best-known feature – the octagonal Spa House – is shown at the top of this 1956 Ordnance Survey map. The house was built in 1830, but the health-giving properties of the sulphurous water had been originally discovered in the early years of the previous century.

At the bottom of the map, with a long tree-lined entrance drive off Nottington Lane stands Nottington House. This fine mansion was built in 1817 for the local Tucker Steward family who owned it until around 1930, when it was sold. The house saw use an Anti-Aircraft Gun Operations Centre during the Second World War and in the grounds can be seen the huts used to accommodate the wartime military. By the time the map was produced they had become home for a number of local families displaced by wartime bombing raids and continued to be used, although not really fit for the purpose, until the early 1960s.

Nottington House was demolished in 1967. The apartments of Nottington Court now stand here, close to but not on the exact 'footprint' of the old house.

Nottington Spa House in the early 1900s.

Nottington House, demolished in 1967.

The Spa House today.

Nottington Court, apartments built in the grounds of Nottington House.

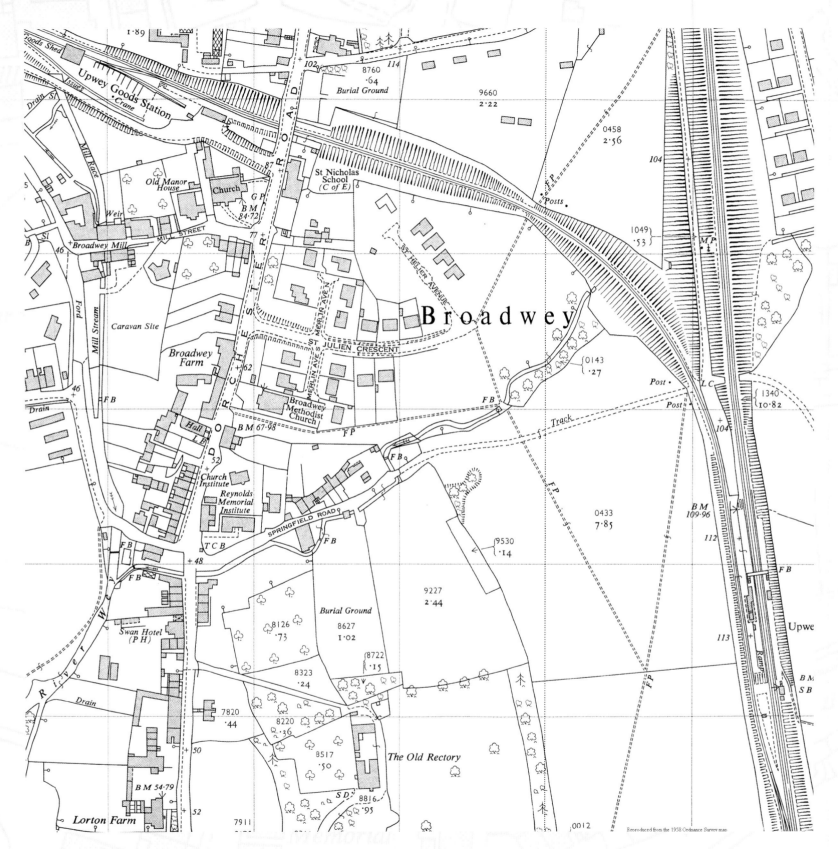

Upwey Goods Station

Goods Shed

1·89

Drain Sl

Issues

Mill Race

Church

Old Manor House

Weir

Broadwey Mill

B·Sl

MILL STREET

46

Ford

Mill Stream

Caravan Site

Broadwey Farm

DORCHESTER ROAD

G P

BM 84·72

77

62

St Nicholas School (C of E)

87

102

8760 ·64

Burial Ground

114

ST HELIER AVENUE

MERLIN AVE S

ST JULIEN CRESCENT

9660 2·22

0458 2·56

FP Posts

104

1049 ·53

MP

B r o a d w e y

0143 ·27

Post

Post

LC

1340 10·82

104

Broadwey Methodist Church

FB

Track

FP

FB

Drain

FB

Hall LB

52

BM 67·98

FP

FB

Church Institute

Reynolds Memorial Institute

SPRINGFIELD ROAD

FB

TCB

0433 7·85

BM 109·96

112

9530 ·14

FB

48

9227 2·44

FB

FB

River Wey

Swan Hotel (P H)

8126 ·73

Burial Ground

8627 1·02

8722 ·15

8323 ·24

113

Upwe

B M

S B

Drain

7820 ·44

8220 ·36

8517 ·50

The Old Rectory

FP

Ramp

BM 54·79

50

Lorton Farm

52

7911

S D

8816 ·95

0012

MAP 56

ORDNANCE SURVEY 1958 : BROADWEY

On the main line, bottom right of this map, is the present Upwey and Broadwey railway station, formerly known as Upwey Junction when it served the Abbotsbury branch line which heads off to the west on the map. The Abbotsbury Branch closed to passengers in 1952 and after that only Upwey Station on its line remained in use as Upwey Goods Station until it finally closed in 1962. Railway buildings still stand, now used by a local building firm (Buildrite) and a coal merchant (Restoricks). Although situated in Broadwey, the railway station's original Broadwey name led to confusion with another station, Broadway in Worcestershire, so 'Upwey' was chosen instead.

Apart from land around 'The Old Rectory' almost the whole of the area shown between Dorchester Road and the main railway line has been filled with houses. The Reynolds Memorial Institute opened in 1933, built with money left by Broadwey resident Frank Reynolds.

On the opposite side of Dorchester Road the Swan Inn has since closed, the 'Hall' at No. 619 dates from 1878 when it was used for meetings of the Temperance Movement and the former Broadwey Farm is now a private house. The building opposite St Nicholas church was still a school in 1958 but its pupils combined with those from Upwey in 1972 and moved to a new site, their former building then being converted to housing.

St Nicholas church, Broadwey, much altered and extended since John Upham published his engraving in 1825.

Looking south down a very rural Dorchester Road in the late-nineteenth century. Broadwey Farm is prominent in the background and in the foreground, the house on the corner of Mill Street and Dorchester Road is recognisable today by its small bay window.

MAP 57

ORDNANCE SURVEY 1927 (with 1938 additions) : UPWEY

Upwey is a long village, stretching down Church Street from St Laurence church, past the old village school, the Wishing Well, and the turnings to Elwell Street (*see* MAP 58) and Stottingway Street, which both lead out on to Dorchester Road, quieter now that the traffic to Dorchester takes the route of the new Relief Road. (*See* MAP 59 *for a 1959 view of the now defunct hairpin bend on the A354*)

At the northern end of the village stands Batchfoot House, once the Rectory and now a residential home. The church of St Laurence dates back at least to the fifteenth century and long before that a little Chantry was founded in Upwey in 1243 by John Bayouse, whose surname led to Upwey's alternative name of 'Waibaiouse'. Another church building in the street is now converted to residential use, but was formerly a Methodist church, built in 1809. The village school closed in 1976 but is still in use as a village community centre.

The village has a very fine mill. When Thomas Hardy was asked on which mill 'Overcombe Mill' in his novel *The Trumpet Major* was based, he replied that it was a composite picture of two local mills – Upwey and Sutton Poyntz.

Church Street, Upwey, with, on the extreme left, a glimpse of the Wishing Well. The church of St Laurence is in the background.

The Wishing Well and English's tea garden, a popular destination for horse and carriage excursions from Weymouth in the early 1900s, and still a tourist attraction today.

A snow-clad St Laurence church in about 1910.

Dorchester Road, Upwey in the early 1900s.

Upwey Mill still stands in Church Street, although some years have elapsed since corn was milled here.

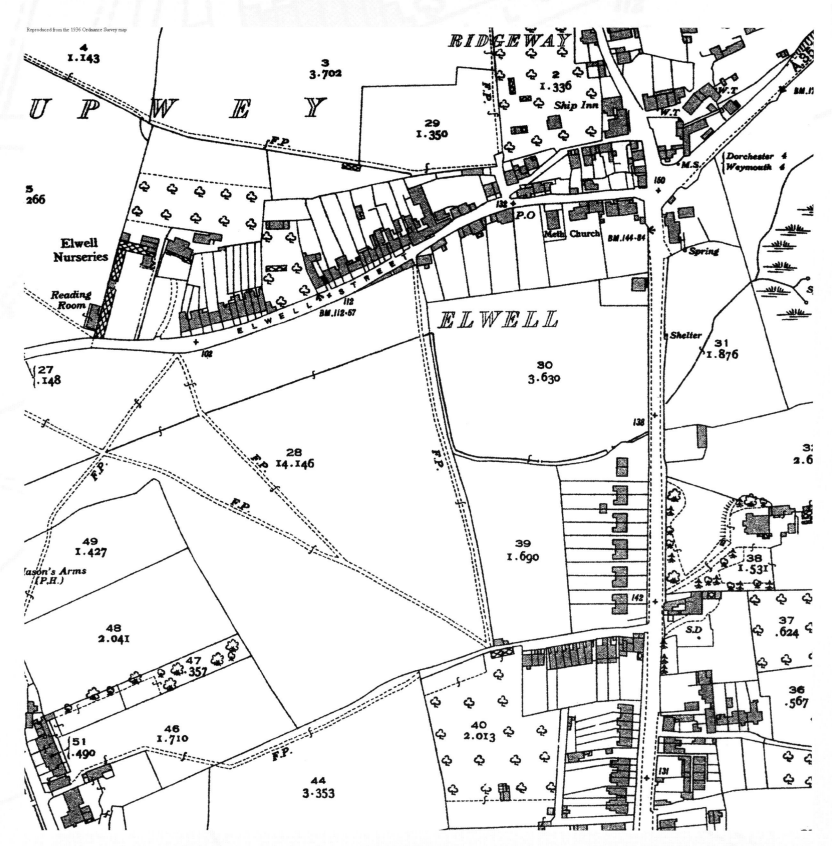

RIDGEWAY

U P W E Y

4
1.143

3
3.702

29
1.350

2
1.336

Ship Inn

W.T

W.T

BM.12

Dorchester 4
Weymouth 4

M.S

150

P.O

Meth. Church

BM.144·84

Spring

Elwell
Nurseries

Reading
Room

ELWELL STREET

112

BM.112·57

ELWELL

102

Shelter

31
1.876

27
.148

30
3.630

138

28
14.146

33
2.6

FP.

FP.

FP.

FP.

49
1.427

39
1.690

38
1.531

142

48
2.041

Mason's Arms
(P.H.)

S.D

37
.624

47
.352

36
.567

46
1.710

40
2.013

51
.490

FP.

131

44
3.353

MAP 58
ORDNANCE SURVEY 1936 : UPWEY

Elwell Street is the link between Church Street and the foot of Ridgeway. Prior to the opening of the 'new road' in 1824 (top right of the map), the way to Dorchester was via the steep 'Old Roman Road' passing the Ship Inn. The 1824 road had easier gradients but introduced the hairpin bend at the junction to Bincombe, the scene of many accidents since coming of the motor car. (*See* MAP 59 *for more details of the hairpin bend and 2011 Relief Road*).

The stone plaque which commemorates one of the Reverend Gildea's gifts to the village in the early twentieth century. In place now for almost a century and rather weathered by time, it reads '*By the generosity and untiring efforts of the Rev. Canon William Gildea, M.A. (rector of this parish), this approach to Elwell Street was widened and improved entirely at his own expense. His fellow members of the Weymouth Rural District Council desire thus to place on record their appreciation of the great interest he has always taken in this parish. October, 1917.*'

A print made in 1821, based on one of John Upham's paintings, shows the view from Dorchester Road with some of the houses in Elwell Street on the right.

Today, Elwell Street is largely residential but in 1936 when the map was produced it had much more of a real 'village street' character and memories of those who lived there bring the area to life.

On Elwell Street's northern side the first cottage once had an area where the village bier was stored. Next to it Canon William Gildea, Rector of Upwey from 1901 until 1922, purchased and demolished two ruined cottages to provide road widening and a village pound for straying animals. A plaque on the wall commemorates his gift. Long-time residents can remember when Elwell Street had a Post Office, a coal merchant, butcher, chip shop, grocery store, market garden and the Elwell Nurseries. A Methodist chapel not far from the Dorchester Road junction has been converted to residential use, as have most of the other properties in the street. At the opposite end of the street the 'Reading Room' is no more – it was established in 1906, another of the gifts of Canon Gildea and the field it stood in was known as 'Reading Field'. As well as a meeting place, the room saw use as a polling station, a World War Two Home Guard base and classroom for evacuees. It was destroyed in a fire in the 1970s.

Elwell Street in 2011.

A number of smaller disused chapel buildings in local villages have been converted to dwellings – this was the Methodist chapel in Elwell Street.

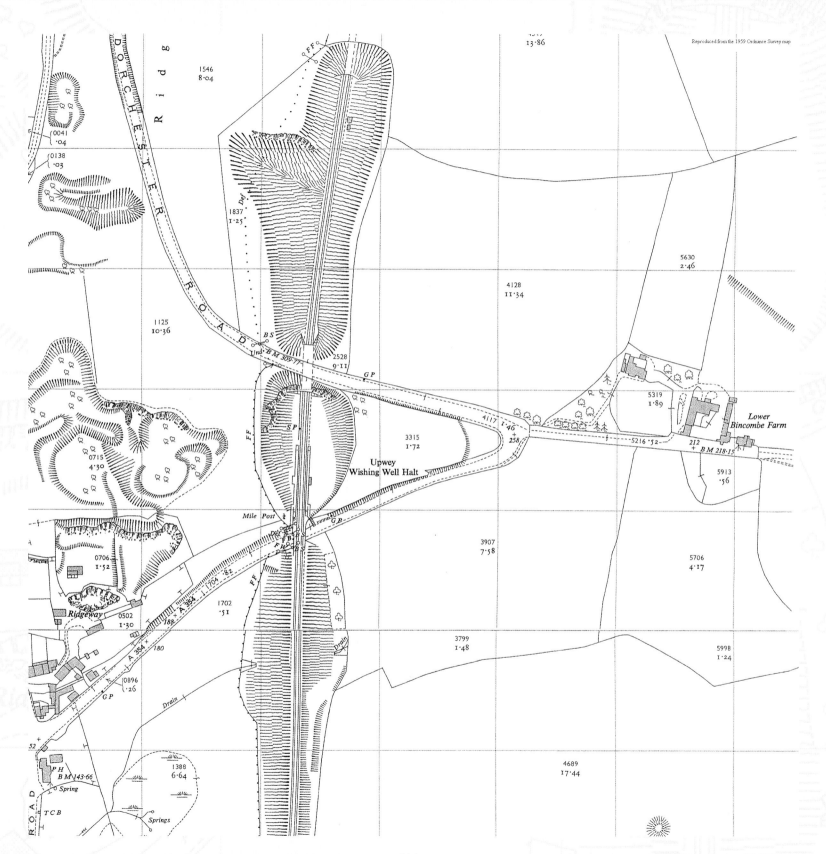

DORCHESTER ROAD

Ridg

1546
8·04

0041
·04

0138
·03

1125
10·36

0715
4·30

0706
I·52

0502
I·30

Ridgeway

0896
·26

52

PH
BM I43·66

Spring

TCB

ROAD

Springs

1388
6·64

1837
I·25

Def

BS
Und·BM 309·77

2528
9·11

FF

SP

Mile Post

Du

FB

FH·S

1704·82

A·354

188

A·354 180

1702
·51

GP

Drain

GP

3315
I·72

Upwey
Wishing Well Halt

4117

258

I·46

4128
II·34

3907
7·58

3799
I·48

13·86

5630
2·46

5319
I·89

5216·52

212
BM 218·15

Lower
Bincombe Farm

5913
·56

5706
4·17

5998
I·24

4689
I7·44

Drain

MAP 59

ORDNANCE SURVEY 1959 : UPWEY

Since 2009 locals have watched the new Weymouth Relief Road taking shape and following its completion, the prominent feature of this 1959 map has disappeared – the hairpin bend on Ridgeway Hill, with its sharp turning leading down to Bincombe village. The road was cut in the early 1820s to replace the former route to Dorchester via the steep 'Old Roman Road' leading out of Upwey at the bottom of the hill.

John Upham's 1825 engraving is of the new 1824 'hairpin bend' road out of Upwey. More than 180 years later, great swathes of white chalk were visible once again as the Relief Road of 2011 advanced across the Ridgeway.

Upwey Wishing Well Halte.

With the closure of this section of the A354 road, one of the causes of not infrequent hold-ups here has ended. Another cause of traffic tailbacks was the occasional failure of lorry drivers to appreciate the low height of the railway bridge just below the bend. Any large vehicle unable to pass beneath the bridge required a lengthy police-controlled reversing procedure before being able to find sufficient space to turn and be re-routed.

The Relief Road was officially opened by Princess Anne on 10th December 2010, although weather conditions delayed its final completion and opening to traffic until 17th March 2011.

Upwey Wishing Well Halte (the spelling was a GWR tradition) opened in 1905 and steps adjacent to the bridge led down to the main road. The halt was probably given this name to distinguish it from other local stations with Upwey in their names – although anyone alighting here would have a long, long walk to the little tourist attraction in Church Street! The Wishing Well halt closed in January 1957.

The railway bridge over the A354 road at Upwey.

A serious accident at the hairpin bend in 1922 resulted in many injuries and the death of one passenger when this charabanc left the road. It was returning from a Bank Holiday outing.

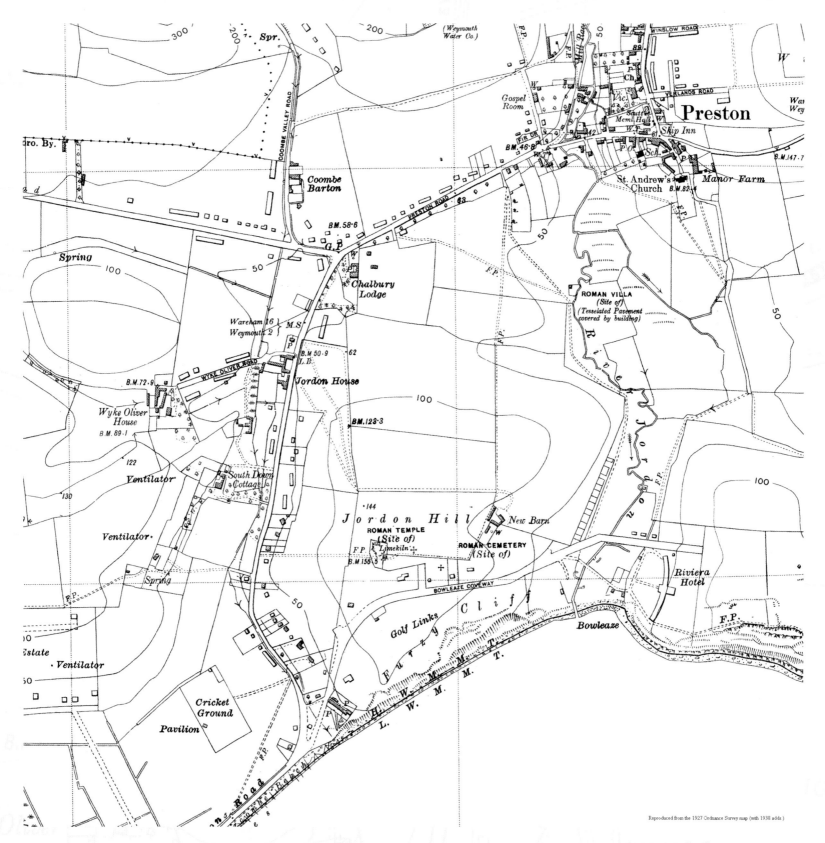

118

MAP 60

ORDNANCE SURVEY 1927 (with 1938 revisions) : PRESTON

Quite a rural scene at Overcombe Corner on this Ordnance Survey map of 1927 (with some 1938 revision).

Two sporting venues can be seen – Lodmoor Cricket Ground, which was on land formerly used as an airfield and, on the other side of Preston Road, are Golf Links – this area was to be presented to the town as a public open space in 1955 by Mr and Mrs A. J. Mayne – he had been one of the agents of the Weymouth Bay Estate Company (*see* MAP 61). Bowleaze Coveway had been laid out by the Company, but the Riviera Hotel was not part of the plan – it opened in 1932 as a quite separate and independent development and is one of the additions to the original 1927 map.

Apart from houses strung out along Preston Road (often referred to then as 'the Bournemouth Road') there is little in the way of development on either side of it, most of the streets built here dating from the 1950s and later. Chalbury Corner takes its name from Chalbury Lodge, home for many years of the local Scutt family. Both locations owe their name to Chalbury Hill Fort, the Iron Age fortification which overlooks the villages here. The Roman Temple site off Bowleaze Coveway is open to view.

To the west and unnamed on the map, is Littlemoor Road, which in earlier times was known as 'Seven Gates Road'. It leads to today's ever growing suburb of Littlemoor, the first developments here taking place in the early 1950s. Today Littlemoor, surrounded by beautiful countryside, has grown out of all recognition from that small estate of some sixty years ago.

MAP 62 *shows Preston village in more detail.*

Stormy weather and high seas frequently brought thousands of tons of shingle cascading over the Preston Beach Wall, blocking the road and disrupting traffic.

Bowleaze Cove, a photograph from the 1920s.

The problem was solved when the massive new Preston beach sea defences were completed in 1996, and the new wall has extended the Esplanade to Overcombe.

The Riviera building before an additional storey of chalets was added each side of the tower. This 1930s art deco design is now a listed building.

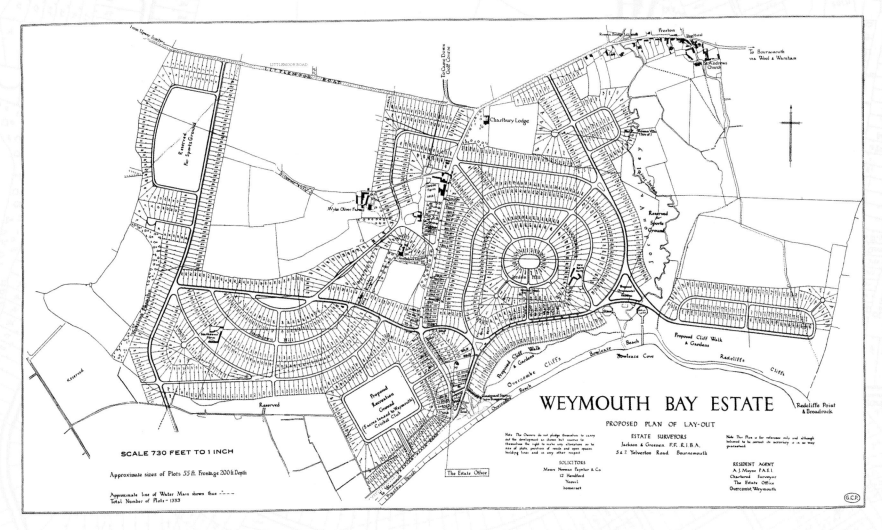

WEYMOUTH BAY ESTATE

PROPOSED PLAN OF LAY-OUT

SCALE 730 FEET TO 1 INCH

Approximate sizes of Plots 55 ft. Frontage 200 ft. Depth

Approximate line of Water Main shown thus -----
Total Number of Plots = 1333

ESTATE SURVEYORS
Jackson & Greenen. F.F. R.I.B.A.
5 & 7 Yelverton Road. Bournemouth

SOLICITORS
Messrs Norman Paynter & Co.
12 Hendford
Yeovil
Somerset

RESIDENT AGENT
A. J. Mayne P.A.S.I.
Chartered Surveyor
The Estate Office
Overcombe, Weymouth

Reserved for Sports Ground

Charlbury Lodge

Proposed Recreation Ground
(5 acres leased to Weymouth Cricket Club)

Reserved

The Estate Office

Proposed Cliff Walk & Gardens

Overcombe Cliffs

Bowleaze Cove

Redcliffe Cliffs

Redcliffe Point & Broadrock

Bowleaze Cove in 2011.

MAP 61

THE WEYMOUTH BAY ESTATE PLAN, late 1920s : PRESTON

Very ambitious proposals were put forward in the late 1920s for the development of large tracts of land on either side of Preston Road. Here, the Weymouth Bay Estate Company planned to erect well over one thousand dwellings, on individual plots each estimated to have a frontage of 55 feet and a depth of 200 feet.

Had the plan been carried through, houses would have been built around what was then Lodmoor Cricket Ground, along today's Beachdown Way, Preston Beach Road and northwards along Preston Road, from where a new road would head west to link to a crescent pattern of streets. From here another planned road was join Littlemoor Road where more houses were to enclose an intended Sports Ground.

East of Preston Road the company's plans, if carried through, would have seen the whole of Jordan Hill densely covered with houses. Along Preston Road some of the planned development did take place and the estate's first new road, Bowleaze Coveway, was laid out, although it was much shorter than envisaged. If the original plan had been followed, houses would have extended along it from Bowleaze as far as Redcliff Point.

Work on the Weymouth Bay Estate ceased in the early 1930s – probably due to the severe economic situation, soon followed by the outbreak of World War Two. Roads branching off Preston Road are developments of the 1950s and later, while some of the planned housing land is now the site of holiday camps.

The long walkway along the 1996 Preston Beach wall and sea defences links with the Esplanade at Greenhill.

Above and right: Contrasting views of Overcombe Corner in the 1930s and 2011.

The map denotes 'supposed Roman Bridge' at Preston, but this is now thought to be a mediaeval pack horse bridge.

Climbing up the main road out of Preston, with the Ship Inn (now the Spice Ship) on the right. The cottages on the left were removed for road improvements here in the 1960s.

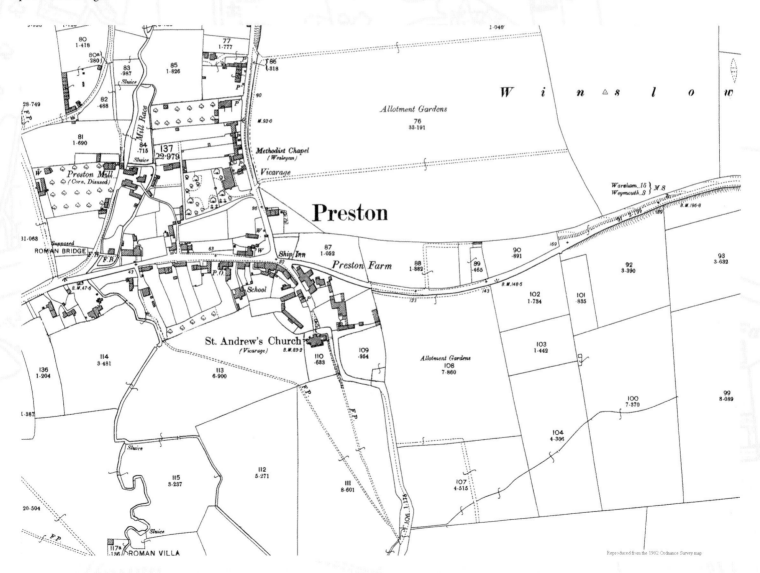

MAP 62

ORDNANCE SURVEY 1902 and 1938 : PRESTON

Preston is the most easterly of the parishes which were brought within the borough boundary in 1933. Thirty six years apart, these two maps illustrate some increase in the number of dwellings in the village, but the major housing developments later in the twentieth century would be to the north and west of the old settlement. Flowing through the village and entering the sea at Bowleaze Cove is the much-diverted River Jordan, which once supported Preston's corn mill, demolished long ago, although the mill house still stands.

Today Preston is probably best known for the holiday caravans which line up in rows across its fields, but this is an area with much history. Sadly, though, the tessellated pavement of the Roman Villa shown on the maps cannot be seen today. Discovered in 1902, it was unfortunately a well-publicised site and early visitors made off with its mosaics as souvenirs, leading to what remained of it being covered over.

Famous names connected with Preston include John Wesley, much persecuted in the seventeenth century for his non-conformist views and grandfather of Methodism's John and Charles Wesley. In the early nineteenth century, visitor John Constable, on honeymoon in Osmington, made sketches in Preston church.

Development of two roads east of the village took place between the dates of these two maps – Verlands Road (probably deriving its name from 'furlong') and Winslow Road, an old name for lands here.

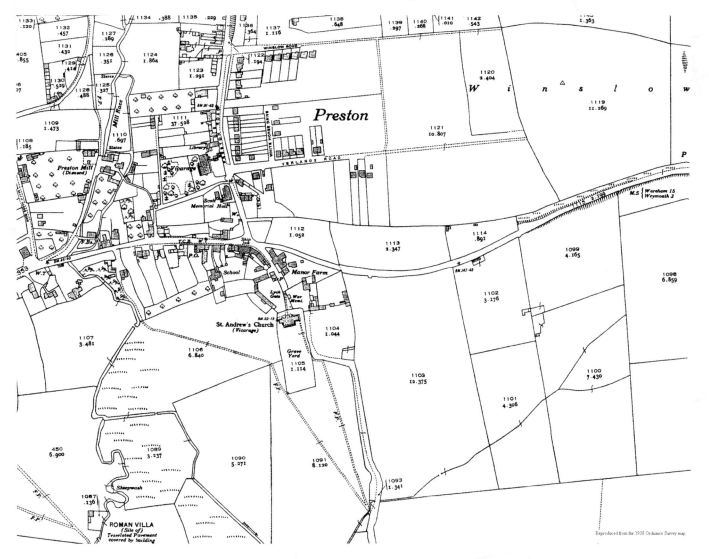

Reproduced from the 1938 Ordnance Survey map

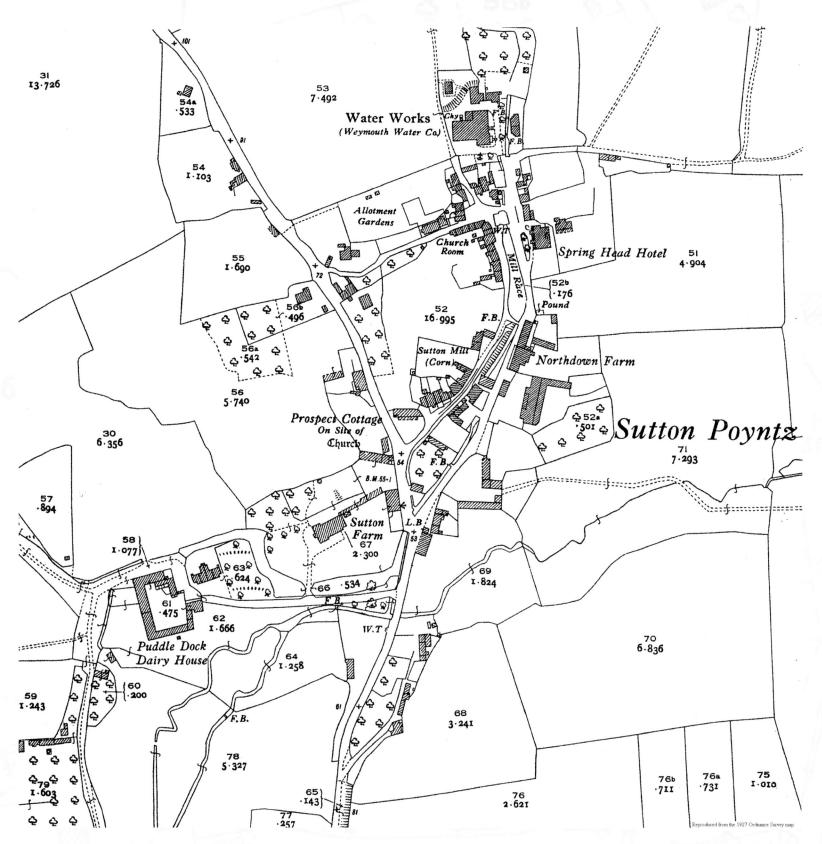

MAP 63

ORDNANCE SURVEY 1927 : SUTTON POYNTZ

'Boiling Rock' the descriptively named spring at Sutton Poyntz was the source of the first piped water supply to Melcombe Regis in 1797 (Weymouth had to wait quite a lot longer). Eminent Victorian engineer Thomas Hawksley designed the original water works buildings shown on the map, which were later extended.

A pumping station is still in operation here and the buildings now also house a Museum of Water Supply. 'Sutton' of the village's name means 'southern settlement' and 'Poyntz' is the family name of mediaeval lords of the manor. Written records of the village in the mediaeval period are slight and there is nothing to suggest that any members of this important family lived here, although they are known to have made occasional visits. Although Sutton was at one time the principal settlement, Preston now has the much larger population and – since the fourteenth or fifteenth century – the parish church.

The map indicates that an ecclesiastical building stood on or near the site of 'Prospect Cottage' and it has long been thought that this was a mediaeval chapel. In 1993 Wessex Archaeology excavated a site to the north west of the water works (just beyond the top of this map) prior to the building of new water treatment works. The mediaeval walls and artefacts found suggest manorial buildings and possibly a chapel once stood on this site so there is still some uncertainty as to exact location or locations of any early religious buildings.

An ecclesiastical building of much later date, the Roman Catholic church of Our Lady, occupied a converted building almost opposite the entrance to Puddledock Lane in post-World War Two years.

Today, as the River Jordan meanders through it, Sutton Poyntz is peaceful and picture-postcard pretty, with far fewer modern buildings than neighbouring Preston.

Sutton Poyntz's Springhead Hotel, and, in the background the tall chimney of the Weymouth Waterworks Company's pumping station. Redundant after the introduction of electric pumps, the chimney was taken down in 1979.

Sutton Mill on the left faces a row of cottages destroyed by fire on the 18th April 1908.

The view from the opposite direction as Weymouth Fire Brigade attempt to damp down smouldering thatched buildings after the fire.

It is hard to believe that these pretty thatched cottages fell into such ruin that in the 1950s they were described as a disgrace and an eyesore and the pond they stood beside became weed-choked and mosquito-ridden.

Today the village is back to being picture-postcard perfect once more.

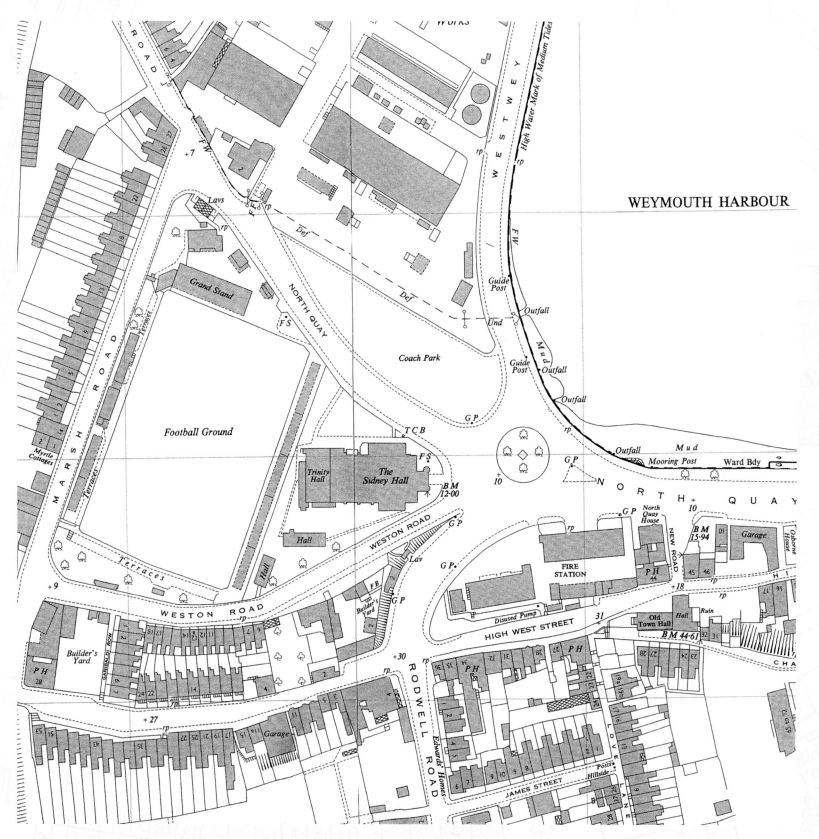

WEYMOUTH HARBOUR

MAP 64

ORDNANCE SURVEY 1958 WEYMOUTH : North Quay

A return to Weymouth for the final selection of maps, all taken from the 50″ = 1 mile Ordnance Survey of the 1950s, most of which have been reduced in scale. This view of North Quay and Westwey Road has seen much change over the past half century. The Sidney Hall and Football Ground gave way in the late 1980s to the Asda supermarket and its car parks. A large apartment block – Spinnaker View – now stands at the entrance to Weston Road. Westwey House was built on the former coach park and gas works site in 1972, although later alterations have completely altered its original façade. The old 'disused pump' at the rear of the Fire Station has been moved to Hope Square and the fire station buildings will soon be empty as work on the new building in Radipole Lane nears completion (2011).

The roundabout at the bottom of Boot Hill (Rodwell Road) was replaced by controversial traffic lights in 2010-11, part of the pre-2012 Olympic Games Weymouth Transport Package. (*Compare this map with* MAPS 19, 37 *and* 38)

The Weymouth Transport Package roadworks of 2010-2011 have brought about the demise of three town roundabouts and their not (as yet) altogether welcome replacement with traffic lights – this one on North Quay (now known as Harbour Crossroads), one at the end of Westwey Road (now known as Westham Crossroads, a name formerly used by locals for the junction of Abbotsbury Road and Chickerell Road) and a third at the end of King Street.

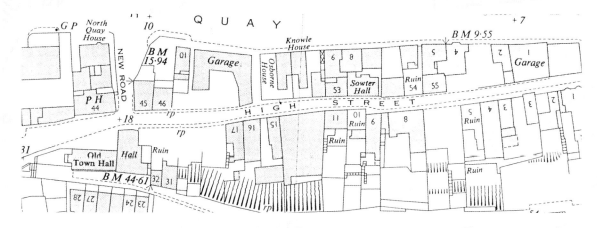

North Quay and High Street buildings which were cleared in 1961 to make way for the 1971 Municipal Offices and its car parks.
The Tudor House was No. 4 North Quay.

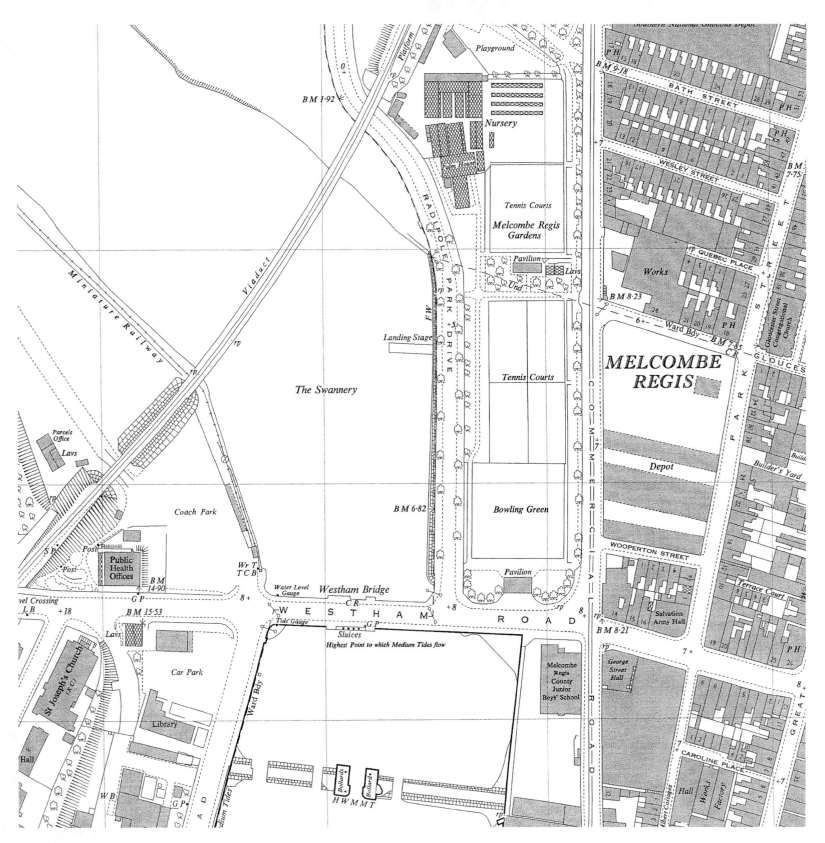

Playground

Nursery

BM 1·92

Viaduct

Platform

0 +

BM 9·18

P H

BATH STREET

WESLEY STREET

BM 7·75

QUEBEC PLACE

Works

Tennis Courts

Melcombe Regis Gardens

Pavilion

Lavs

Und

BM 8·23

Ward Bdy

BM 7·85

6 +

CR

GLOUCE

Gloucester Street Congregational Church

Miniature Railway

rp

rp

FW

Landing Stage

RADIPOLE PARK DRIVE

The Swannery

Tennis Courts

MELCOMBE REGIS

Depot

Builder's Yard

Buildi

rp

Parcels Office

Lavs

BM 6·82

Bowling Green

COMMERCIAL

Pavilion

WOOPERTON STREET

Terrace Court

Coach Park

S P

Post

Post

Post

Public Health Offices

BM 14·90

Wr T
T C B

Water Level Gauge

Westham Bridge

CR

GP

8 +

WESTHAM

Salvation Army Hall

BM 8·21

rp

7 +

ROAD

8 +

rp

el Crossing
L B

+18

BM 15·53

Lavs

Car Park

Tide Gauge

Sluices

GP

Highest Point to which Medium Tides flow

Melcombe Regis County Junior Boys' School

George Street Hall

ROAD

8 +

St Joseph's Church
(R C)

Library

Ward Bdy

Hall

Works Factory

CAROLINE PLACE

7 +

GREAT

7 +

Hall

W B

GP

Bollards

Bollards

H W M M T

Medium Tides

rp

128

MAP 65

ORDNANCE SURVEY 1956 WEYMOUTH : Westham Bridges

Of the three structures shown here crossing Weymouth Backwater, only one remains – Westham Bridge of 1921, and it is now closed to traffic and used as a car park. Below it is the long-disused Victorian dam, intended to control the flow of water in the days when sewage was dumped in the Backwater. The sewage problem was tackled around the turn of the twentieth century and since 1921 the current bridge with its sluices has controlled the water flow. The redundant dam was removed in 1995 when the present Marina was developed. Above the bridge, the viaduct of the Weymouth and Portland Railway was removed in 1974-6, the railway having finally closed in 1965. Buildings and land use on both sides of the harbour have changed greatly – some of these developments are illustrated below. (*Compare this map with* MAP 22)

Weymouth Library's 'temporary' prefab building of 1948 was replaced by the present town centre building in 1990. Flats which now stand here are illustrated on page 45.

Looking south, an aerial view of the map opposite taken in 1972. Car parking had already taken over the tennis courts north of Westham Bridge. The disused railway viaduct was removed in 1974-5 and the Swannery Road bridge of 1987 now crosses the water here.

Compare this illustration of the Harbour Tramway railway line in 1910 with the amount of reclaimed land shown on the map opposite. The tramway lines run down the centre of the aerial photograph, and down the centre of Commercial Road on the map.

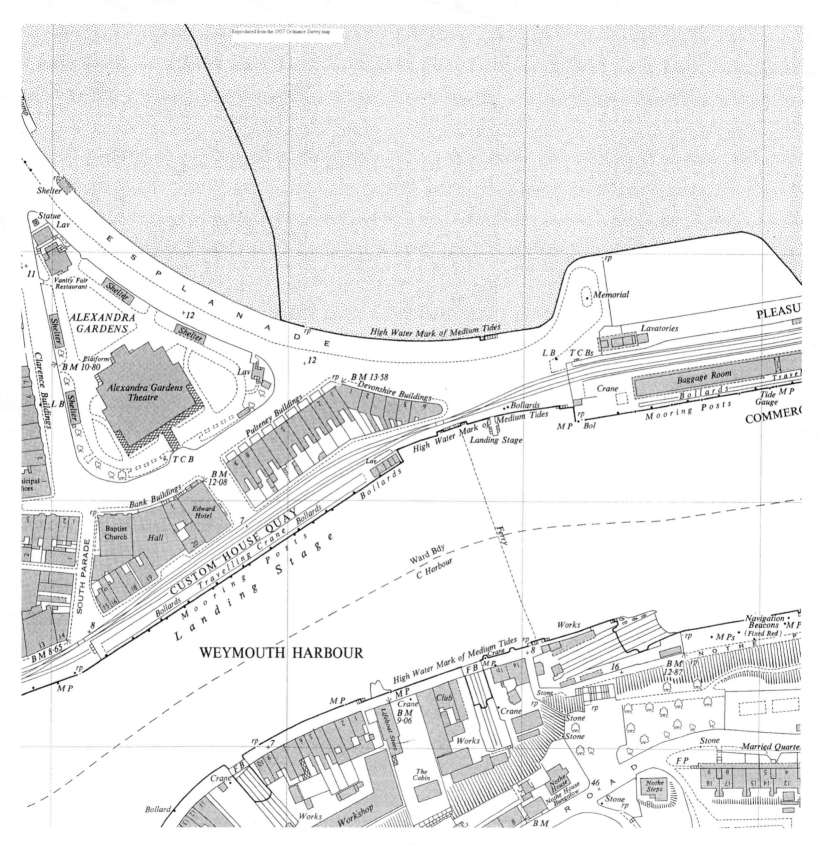

Shelter

Statue
Lav

Vanity Fair
Restaurant

ESPLANADE

+11

Shelter

+12

ALEXANDRA
GARDENS

Shelter

Memorial

PLEASU

Shelter

Platform
BM 10·80

Lav

+12

High Water Mark of Medium Tides

Lavatories

Clarence Buildings

L B

L B

Alexandra Gardens
Theatre

BM 13·58

Devonshire Buildings

T C Bs

Crane

Baggage Room

Travel

Bollards

Pulteney Buildings

Bollards

High Water Mark of Medium Tides

Mooring Posts

Tide M P
Gauge

COMMERC

TCB

Lav

MP Bol

Landing Stage

MP

nicipal
fices

BM
12·08

Bank Buildings

Edward
Hotel

Baptist
Church

Hall

CUSTOM HOUSE QUAY

Travelling Crane Bollards

Bollards

High Water Mark of Medium Tides

Landing Stage

Mooring Posts

SOUTH PARADE

Ferry

Ward Bdy
C Harbour

Navigation
Beacons · M P
(Fixed Red)

Works

rp

· M Ps

BM 8·65

+8

Bollards

Landing Stage

WEYMOUTH HARBOUR

High Water Mark of Medium Tides

Crane

+8

16 +

BM
12·87

NOTHE

MP

F B M P

Stone

Stone

MP
BM
9·06

Crane

Club

Crane

Works

Stone

Stone

Crane

Lifeboat Store

Works

Stone

Married Quarte

+7

The
Cabin

Nothe
House

Nothe House
Bungalow

46 +

FP

Nothe
Steps

F B

Crane

Bollard

Works

Workshop

Stone

B M

130

MAP 66

ORDNANCE SURVEY 1957 WEYMOUTH : Esplanade

In 1957 the empty area shown on the map alongside the Pleasure Pier had been the site of the 1908 Pavilion Theatre, renamed The Ritz in 1950, and destroyed by fire on 13th April 1954. Much legal wrangling followed and it was 1960 before the present Pavilion Theatre opened here.

Infilling has since completely changed the shape of the Pier. The 1889 Baggage Room, extended in the 1930s, was replaced in 1967 by a passenger terminal, customs hall and offices.

The Alexandra Gardens Theatre also fell victim to fire, in September 1993 and an amusement complex – the Electric Palace – has replaced it.

The Pier in 1939...

...and 1979.

The Pavilion (later The Ritz) Theatre 1908-1954.

The Pavilion Theatre of 1960.

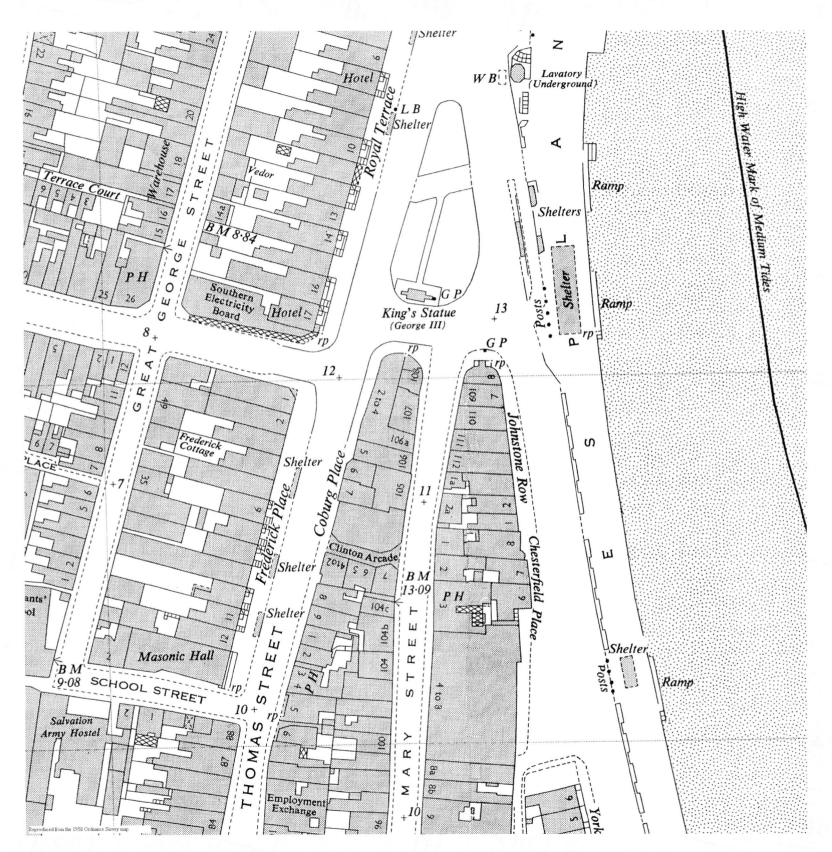

N

A

Shelter

W B

Lavatory
(Underground)

L B
Shelter

Hotel

Royal Terrace

Ramp

Shelters

Terrace Court

Warehouse

GREAT GEORGE STREET

24

22

16

20

18

17 16 15

9 5 4 3

Vedor

BM 8.84

14a

10

13

14

16

Southern
Electricity
Board

PH

Hotel

25 26

King's Statue
(George III)

G P

13

12

11

Ramp

Posts

Shelter

L P

rp

rp

G P

rp

S

E

8+

rp

Frederick
Cottage

Shelter

Shelter

Shelter

FREDERICK PLACE

THOMAS STREET

Coburg Place

Clinton Arcade

Masonic Hall

BM
9.08

SCHOOL STREET

rp

10+

+7

35

Employment
Exchange

Salvation
Army Hostel

ants'
ol

PLACE

108

2 to 4

107

106a

106

105

BM
13.09

104c

104b

104

160

96

Johnstone Row

Chesterfield Place

8

7

109

110

111 112

2a

3

P H

4 to 8

8a

8b

York

9

5

Shelter

Posts

Ramp

+10

MAP 67

ORDNANCE SURVEY 1958 WEYMOUTH : Esplanade
(in its original 50″= 1 mile scale)

The site of Weymouth's King George III statue, the monarch who brought fame to the small seaside town when he spent fourteen holidays here between 1789 and 1805, bringing with him not only his Queen and many of his large family, but also the rich and titled and everyone who wanted to be part of 'Royal Weymouth'. The King on his high Portland stone plinth looks along the Esplanade which he made famous, towards the 'Gloucester Hotel' which was his holiday home and at that time known as 'Royal Lodge' or 'Gloucester Lodge', a name it has reverted to today since it ceased to be a hotel and was converted to apartments. Royal Terrace and to the south of it, Frederick Place stand on the former gardens of the Royal residence. Royal Terrace is minus one of its original houses, No. 18, demolished in the 1920s to widen Westham Road

King George III might well have looked through Harvey's Weymouth Guide Book when he holidayed here in 1800 – its accompanying map (*see* MAP 11) providing a very different townscape from the one illustrated here.

The King's Statue from the 1880s to the present day – the area in front of the monument was once a large open space where crowds gathered to celebrate local and national events. The King never saw the fine houses which stand behind his monument – they were built some years after his final visit and after the statue was unveiled.

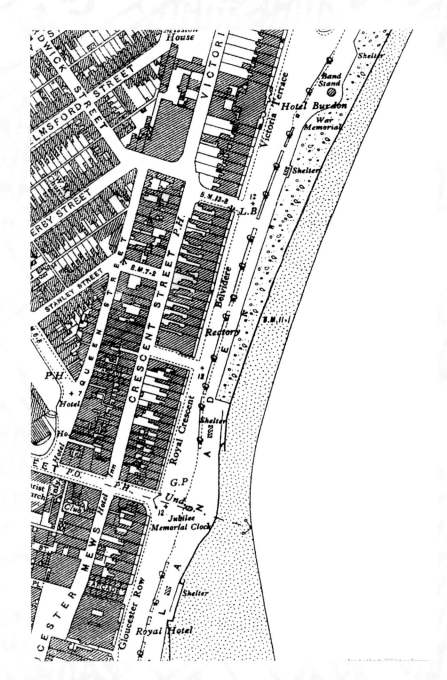

The Jubilee Clock showing the Esplanade widened out around it in the 1920s.

MAP 68

ORDNANCE SURVEY 1927 WEYMOUTH : Esplanade

Stepping back in time, some thirty years prior to the rest of the maps which conclude this book, this 1927 map shows the Esplanade shortly after it was widened out around two structures which once stood on Weymouth beach – the Jubilee Clock and the bandstand opposite the Hotel Burdon (today's Hotel Prince Regent). A walk along the Esplanade today reveals a fascinating collection of monuments and statues which are illustrated here, commemorating events from the sixteenth century to the twentieth.

The Jubilee Clock of 1887 still stands, recently restored, but the bandstand of 1905 was replaced in 1939 (see MAP 69).

Above, from left: The bandstand of 1905, replaced in 1939; Sir Henry Edwards, Victorian Liberal MP and a generous benefactor to the town; The Anzac memorial to the Australian and New Zealand soldiers of World War One, many of whom were wounded at Gallipoli and recuperated in camps locally.

Above, from left: The Clark and Endicott Memorial commemorates sixteenth and seventeenth century voyagers; The 'Great Gale' commemorative stone is now quite worn … and difficult to spot in its Esplanade flowerbed setting; Weymouth War Memorial bears the names of those who gave their lives in World War One and World War Two.

Above, from left: Eric Ricketts was a much respected local architect, author, historian and Freeman of the Borough, who died in 2002; The American Memorial remembers D-Day and the half-million US troops who left Weymouth and Portland for the 1944 invasion of Europe; At the far end of the Esplanade Queen Victoria looks down at the seafront her grandfather King George III made famous, although she never paid any official visits to the town during her long reign.

MAP 69
ORDNANCE SURVEY 1956 WEYMOUTH : Esplanade

The Pier Bandstand of 1939, replacement of the traditional bandstand.

The northern part of Weymouth Esplanade has seen a number of changes since this map was published just over half a century ago. Of its most prominent feature, the Pier Bandstand, only the building on the prom remains today. The open air section, built on piles and projecting into the bay, was demolished in 1986. It had replaced a traditional seaside bandstand in 1939.

At the top of the map St John's School closed in 1972 when replacement buildings opened in Coombe Avenue. 'Greenhill Garage' opposite the school was a more recently redeveloped site when an apartment block went up in its place.

Victoria Terrace was completed in 1855, its restrained style complementing the earlier terraces to the south. The 'Hotel Burdon' is today's Hotel Prince Regent.

Behind the Esplanade, in Victoria Street, the 'County Garage' shown was owned by Tilleys, a firm still in business in the town. The garage was demolished in 1982, by which time it was owned by Wadham Stringer. The flats of Nightingale Court now fill the site. Royal Crescent Surgery was built on the empty site shown just south of it.

St John's School.

Tilley's Garage.

Nightingale Court, the garage's replacement.

The apartment block which replaced St John's School.

CRANFORD AVENUE

Branscombe Hove-Dene St. Hilary Cranford Track

BM 17·28

+ 22

+ 11

+ 16

+ 15

+ 18

Rectory

+ 22

rp

BM 12·42

Peter Pan

Cambrai Town Field

23

Christian Science Church

BM 27·45

Bowling

Lav

FS

Pav

Lav

18

MELCOMBE AVENUE

Tennis Courts

33

+

BM 36·36

Tennis Courts

Bathing Bungalows

Wr T

Tennis Courts

+ 28

BM 29·03

rp

· S D

Nurses' Home

rp

ourts

Surgery

BM 45·53

40

Putting Green

GREENHILL GARDENS

Tennis Court

GREENHILL

Bathing Bungalows

Wr T

High Water Mark of Medium Tides

Low Water Mark of Medium Tides

WEYMOUTH AND DISTRICT HOSPITAL
(General)

F S

27 +

+ 44

rp

Monument

Wr T

Royal Eye Infirmary

Shelter
· S D

Floral Clock

WESTERHALL ROAD

BM 17·36

rp

+ 22

Surgery

BM 35·44

37 +

P

A

R

A

D

E

E

S

P

L

A

N

A

D

E

T C B

Reproduced from the 1957 Ordnance Survey map

138

MAP 70

ORDNANCE SURVEY 1957 : WEYMOUTH : Esplanade

Greenhill Gardens were laid out in the 1870s by Sir Frederic Johnstone and were initially the scene of some disorder when locals destroyed fences and gates, claiming that this was common land: a court case in 1886 found in Sir Frederic's favour and he eventually presented the Gardens to the town as a Coronation gift in 1902. The 'Bathing Bungalows' of the 1920s and '30s shown below the Tennis Courts were due to be replaced, but have now been saved, with Grade 2 listed status.

Weymouth and District Hospital 1902-1998.

Christian Science church of 1929... and its successor Weymouth Bay Methodist church of 2009.

Some named buildings no longer exist: Weymouth and District Hospital buildings of 1902 were demolished following the opening of the new Dorset County Hospital at Dorchester in 1998; the Royal Eye Infirmary on Greenhill is now the Trimar Hospice; the Christian Science church closed in 2004 and was demolished in 2008 to make way for the Weymouth Bay Methodist church, a replacement for Maiden Street Methodist church, gutted by fire in January 2002. The angle of Melcombe Avenue at its northern end led to its original name of 'Bent Path Avenue'.

MAP 71

ORDNANCE SURVEY 1957 : WEYMOUTH : Railway Station

This 1957 map of Weymouth Railway Station was published almost one hundred years after the one of 1864 (MAP 23) and probably its most striking feature is that it shows the amount of land reclaimed from the Backwater in the 1920s and 1930s.

The land originally reclaimed to provide a public park (*see* MAP 14) was north of King Street, although today the Park District is generally thought of as the streets north of Westham Road. On the map, the railway lines shown on the left of the Goods Shed, running north follow the original 'Park Wall' of 1834. All the land west of here was reclaimed in the twentieth century.

At the bottom of the map, in the centre, can be seen the junction of King Street and Commercial Road (the houses at the beginning of Commercial Road are shown as 'Alexandra Terrace' on the 1864 map. In front of the terrace, the roadway and the lines of the Weymouth Harbour Tramway in 1864 directly overlooked the Backwater).

All the land west of Commercial Road on the this map has been reclaimed, some of it as early as 1909 when a much shorter steel viaduct replaced the long timber bridge which formerly took the Weymouth and Portland Railway line across the water to Westham. At the same time the branch railway gained its own station – Melcombe Regis Station – at this end of the line. (Now the site of Swannery Court).

Weymouth Station had undergone a number of changes by 1957 – an extra long platform added alongside Ranelagh Road in 1956 was redundant almost on completion as the steam era was coming to an end with the introduction of diesel locos. The station building had lost its Brunel-style overall timber roof in 1951.

Weymouth's original railway station of 1857.

All the ground shown on the map occupied by Radipole Park Drive and the railway sidings resulted from 1920s' and 1930s' reclamation (the sidings are now the site of Jubilee Retail Park).

Its replacement of 1986.

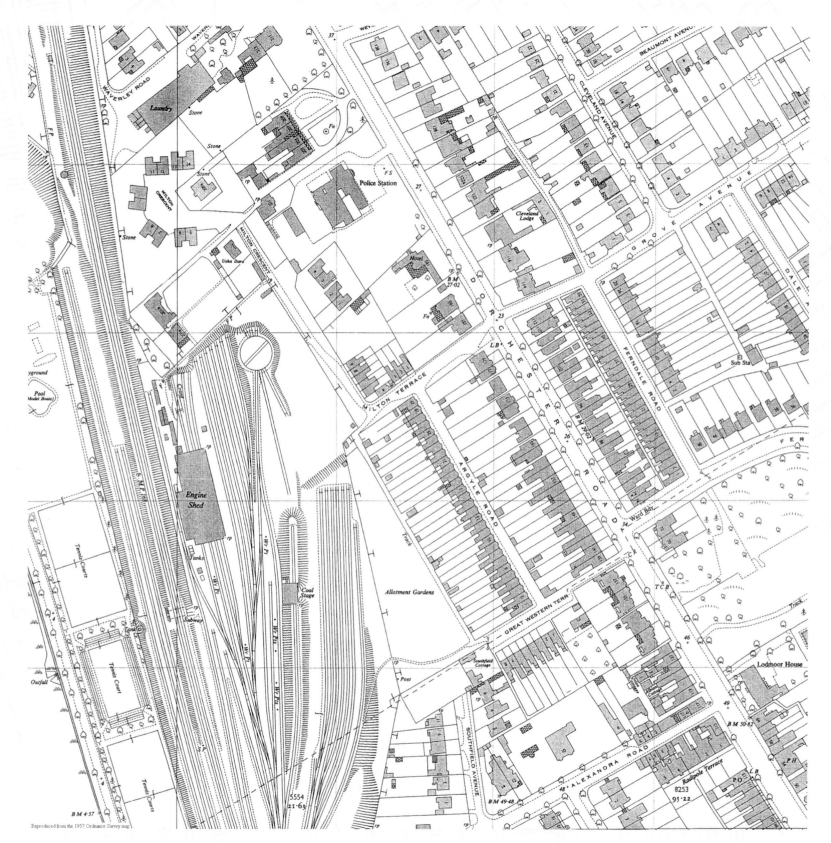

Reproduced from the 1957 Ordnance Survey map

MAP 72

ORDNANCE SURVEY 1957 : WEYMOUTH : Railway Station

A final extract from the 1950s' 50″ = 1 mile maps takes the Weymouth railway station story a little further north and shows the area at the end of the appropriately named Great Western Terrace, a turning off Dorchester Road at Lodmoor Hill.

The last steam regular steam train into Weymouth ran on 9th July 1967 and the Engine Shed, sidings and the turntable would all be gone by 1971. The houses of Lindens Close, Milton Close, Princes Drive, a continuation of Southfield Avenue and Caledonian Close now stand on this former railway land.

The attraction of steam continues and Weymouth now welcomes packed 'Steam Specials' in the summer months. Once the day visitors have been disgorged, it is a little ironic that the loco has to steam back up the track to the Yeovil Railway Centre at Yeovil Junction, now the nearest railway station with a turntable, to be turned around to head the coaches for the return journey from Weymouth in the evening.

Loco 370 at Weymouth in 1893 with the Park District's Brownlow Hotel in the background.

Weymouth Harbour Tramway's Pannier Tank engine 1367 on Custom House Quay.

Proud railwaymen stand beside locomotive 'Windsor Castle' which brought King George VI and the Duke of Kent to Weymouth for the Fleet review of 1938.

Regular visits in the summer months by 'Steam Specials' are hugely popular.

ACKNOWLEDGEMENTS

The majority of the maps and older illustrations reproduced in the book are copied from originals in Weymouth Reference Library's extensive and excellent Local Studies Collection. I am very grateful for Dorset County Library's permission to use them and for the assistance of the ever-helpful staff of Weymouth Library.

My thanks are also due to other organisations, particularly the Ordnance Survey and the United Kingdom Hydrographic Office, whose maps and charts are the main focus of this book.

Sections of aerial photographs on pages 127 and 129 from the Aerofilms collection now in the National Monuments Record are reproduced with the permission of English Heritage. HMS *Osprey* aerial photographs of Ferrybridge (page 89) and Weymouth Pier (page 131) are Crown Copyright and reproduced by permission of the Ministry of Defence. Dorset History Centre allowed me to reproduce a section of an 1844 railway plan (page 39), and Dorset Echo the photograph on page 69 of Maiden Street Methodist Church ablaze.

Barbara Walton kindly gave me permission to reproduce the drawings of Weymouth Town Bridge and the Congregational chapel in West Street (pages 25 and 67) which were made by her father, the late Eric Ricketts. I am indebted to David Gordon Steward for the picture of Nottington House on page 109. Joe Ward captures the changing face of the town with his camera and took the photographs of St John's church (page 41), Nelson's Wharf (page 59), the restored King's Statue (page 133) and the two churches on page 139. Colin Pomeroy's photograph of Broadwey church is on page 111. Brian Jackson took the photographs of Ferry's Corner on page 67 and the Ridgeway railway bridge on page 117 and has, as always, answered my queries about local history matters expertly and patiently. My thanks to everyone.

Other illustrations are from my own collection. I have tried to trace the owners of all original photographs and I apologise for any that I may have failed to acknowledge. Any mistakes in the book are, of course, my own.

I must also thank everyone at Dorset Books/Halsgrove, the publishers of *Weymouth and Portland: Then meets Now*, for their help and patience.

And, once again, my heartfelt thanks for his support to my husband David, whose life and home have once again been taken over by local history.